ENDORSEMENTS
DEVELOl _ _ _ _

"As the owner of a small woman owned business, I felt like this book was written specifically for me. I wish I would have had this book 5 years ago! You included countless examples that I have experienced firsthand (and learned the hard way). You helped to bring together everything that I need to know about developing new business in a logical and efficient manner. This is definitely something I will want as a reference book on my shelf... great advice! I loved the way you summed up the important aspects of each chapter at the end of that chapter and the way certain important points were repeated throughout the book. It was a great way to drive the point home without it feeling redundant. Thank you so much for letting me read the draft! When will I be able to buy my own personal copy?"

—Maureen Nichols, Principal Engineer and owner of ep3inc. Environmental Engineers

"Using her many years of experience in a wide variety of business environments, Sherran has done a masterful job of encapsulating the essential steps associated with developing and maintaining an effective and proven business development strategy. This book will provide the fundamental and mission critical elements associated with driving small business growth via an easy to read, step by step methodology for identifying, developing, and keeping great clients. I have personally worked with Sherran for a number of years and have yet to meet anyone in the consulting industry that shares her level of passion for marketing, business development, and client relations. She is a true professional and the strategies she describes in this book will be of tremendous value to anyone interested in starting a new business or looking to grow an existing enterprise."

—*Walter Reigner, Principal/Manager, AMEC Environment & Infrastructure*

"Business Development, A Guide for the Small Business" is a HOME RUN! Ms. Spurlock discusses the critical elements of implementing a successful business development process for a professional services company. If you're a business owner desiring to take your company to the next level and developing a culture focused on success and winning new projects and clients – this book should be required reading for all employees.

—*Rick Powers, CEO, former BCI Engineers & Scientists, Inc.*

"I've followed Sherran's career for many years (first as a client) and anyone would be wise to follow the advice she has outlined in her book Business Development, A Practical Guide for the Small Professional Services firm."

—*John Wiley, Business Development Manager, URS Corporation*

"Working with Sherran taught us a great deal about business development. She showed us how to be organized in our approach and how to apply polite but persistent follow-up. The results are that we are obtaining great clients and reaping the benefits of those relationships, even many years later. I highly recommend her new book."

—*Janet Hart, President and Owner, Atlanta Environmental Management, Inc.*

"Business Development is a must read for technical, sales, & marketing staff involved in the Professional Services Industry. It is an excellent one stop book that is a complete guide to the Sales process for the Professional Services Industry. From the beginner to the most seasoned in Sales, this book is a winner. Thank you so much for allowing me to read it.

—*Henry Mock, Associate/Business Development, Golder Associates, Inc.*

BUSINESS DEVELOPMENT

A PRACTICAL GUIDE
– FOR THE –
SMALL PROFESSIONAL SERVICES FIRM

SHERRAN S. SPURLOCK

ISBN-10: 1484014383
ISBN-13: 9781484014387

TABLE OF CONTENTS

PREFACE

Why am I writing this book? I see many business owners and good folks out there working hard to bring in new business for their company. I just want to tell them that it really does not need to be so difficult when you understand the right things to do and when to do each of them.

Many people spend hours searching for information online and reading Business Development books authored by so-called experts. Those experts may be great writers or strategic thinkers, or may be perceived experts because of their celebrity name, but have not been in the trenches enough to know the truth and intricacies of how Business Development actually gets done.

The difference with this book is that I've been out there developing new business opportunities for going on thirty years (it doesn't seem possible) and I can tell you what *really* works. I've spent many years educating myself, learning from others and applying what I've learned. I don't claim to know it all—I've just made all the mistakes and learned from them.

My goal with this book is to leverage years of accumulated knowledge to help save you time, resources, and frustration as you grow your business. There's no reason for you to waste time and money trying different tactics in the hopes that the latest idea just might work *this* time.

When I first started out, I could not find a concise resource to help me through the beginnings of my career. My professional degree is in marketing but the training did not prepare me for what I needed to know. I read and studied everything I could, and talked to many people in the business that produced positive results. I learned lessons from their mistakes as well as from the mistakes I made on my own. I'm thankful to say that I've been very successful at marketing professional services, and this book is my way of sharing what I've learned and giving back for all the great years I have enjoyed in this business.

Many of my friends in the business ask me, "Why do you want to give away your secrets?" To begin with, these are not *my* secrets. They are tried and true principles of the trade. I've been using them for years and I know they work when applied at the right point in the process. I'm offering these ideas to anyone that wants to use them.

I've heard things like, "We had to learn it the hard way; let others learn it for themselves." "They won't do it anyway, even if you tell them what to do." "Only when they spend years figuring it out will they do the right thing."

I don't believe that. I believe that the reason you purchased this book is because you know there is a better way and want to learn the correct method for developing new business as early in your career as possible. My goal for these writings is for the information to be a resource that will help you grow your business as fast as you want it to grow.

Another motivation for writing down what I've experienced about Business Development is that I'm watching my friends retire and I see them take away years of accumulated knowledge. It just seems such a waste for the knowledge that we have spent years acquiring to go disappear just because an individual is tired at the end of thirty-five years.

I'm not going to wish you good luck because it is not about luck. It's about doing the right thing at the right time. By having the right knowledge about what needs to be done—you will be prepared to do that!

Recognizing that many people are like me and do not have unlimited hours for reading, I've tried to keep to basics and make the book quick and easy to read. In the pages that follow, I will share with you the step-by-step process necessary for finding new business for your growing company. You will not find sales theory or earth-shattering new concepts—this information is all real-world, tried and true principles.

INTRODUCTION

So! You've started a new business offering professional services of some type. Maybe you have a few good clients, but now you recognize the need to grow the business to the next stage. You are beginning to see that no matter how great you are at what you do, new business will not just walk in the door. You must focus on finding and developing new business opportunities in order to grow your business. Keeping in mind that a small business does not have access to unlimited resources of time and money, this book will show you that the task is not as daunting as it might seem.

You may be a seasoned technical professional who has received a promotion and now has the added responsibility of growing your division or region. Not knowing what to do can be stressful and debilitating, possibly causing you to overanalyze the job. It is not necessary that it be that way when you learn a step-by-step process.

Another goal for this book is to help young technical professionals learn correct basic Business Development skills early in their careers. It is also designed to refresh the skills of seasoned Business Development professionals by providing reminders and new ideas. The information provided can act as motivation to further apply Business Development and marketing skills.

Business Development creates the excitement and the momentum of growth. How Business Development is managed in a company can make the difference between a dynamic growing company and one that continuously struggles to meet payroll. Too many small business owners are overwhelmed, being run by the business instead of enjoying business ownership. The goal is to help you get back to having fun running your own business again!

Topics we will cover:

The Basics of Business Development

To begin, we will discuss the basics of Business Development. Each subsequent chapter will move into more advanced techniques. Business Development is focused on interacting with other people. You can have as many variations as there are different types of people. Everybody has a different idea of how Business Development for professional services should be accomplished. As you will see, there is a specific process that when each step is followed, the desired results will be produced. Use these writings as guidelines and to gather tips on what has worked for many others.

How to Be a "Rainmaker": Attracting New Clients

The "Rainmaker" definition is based on the premise that attracting new clients and building long-term relationships is the most important function of growing a business. Generating new revenue for a professional services company depends on establishing strong long-term relationships.

Business Development Planning and Target Marketing

Building a targeted strategic Business Development plan is the first step in a successful Business Development effort. It sets targets and helps to focus time and dollars where they will be the most effective. When a plan is in place, it is not necessary to stop and think about what should be done for Business Development today or next week. You already know because you have a plan.

Networking Skills

The ability to meet new prospective clients that need your skills can be the lifeblood of any professional services company. We will examine the various types of networking opportunities and determine which will be best for the types of services your business offers.

Client Meetings, Effective Communication and Client Maintenance

While it is hard to argue the value of adding new clients, expanding relationships with *existing* clients and gaining new projects from them can be easier and much less costly. We will discuss critical client retention and verbal communication skills in this segment. An important part of communication is learning to "read" people, so we will also explore the interesting subject of body language.

Proposing Client Solutions

When it comes to proposals, it's not the quantity but the quality that counts. We will discuss a systematic approach geared to help meet the client's specific needs. In addition, we will address how to manage the separate elements of the proposal writing process—even when you have little lead time.

The Winning Short-List Presentation

This segment will include step-by-step instructions for planning, preparing, and delivering quality short-listed presentations, as well as tips, tricks, and shortcuts. Learn how to sell the decision-maker on your concept, make the most of limited presentation time, create a stage presence, manage multiple presenters, choose the best visual aids, communicate effectively, and much more.

Internet Based Marketing and Time Management

Websites and other methods of drawing prospective clients from the Internet can be very effective for professional service firms as long as they are coupled with face-to-face communication.

Time Management

Since time is the most valuable resource we have, we must learn to manage it effectively. Properly conducted internal meetings can help to manage time and productivity.

We will also look at other skills required for the professional services business developer, such as making the telephone work for you, using new technologies, reading people effectively, and recognizing who the true decision-maker is in a group.

What is Business Development?

There is no magic formula to growing sales for the professional services business. Successful Business Development is all based on knowing what to do at the right time. This book will walk you through the steps of setting up a system that can be easily managed because it is designed to open new doors and increase business opportunities. Effective Business Development is not magic; it is a step-by-step process supported by a little hard work.

First of all, evaluate what you have to sell and then identify who will buy your services. From there you must name specific targets and map out a plan for contacting each target. We'll go into more detail on targeting and planning later. It does not need to be complex.

For the small business, marketing and Business Development efforts are sometimes reactive and short-term oriented. The effort is typically in response to a request for a proposal or statement of qualifications. It may be a request to sponsor an event or to become involved in an organization. Maybe it's a group activity or the sudden urge to send out a mailing. All of these may be good ideas, but only if they fit within an overall plan for promoting the business. Otherwise, you can be wasting valuable resources: your time and your money.

Professional services firms differ depending on their service offerings, size and sophistication. Some firms may have advanced to the stage of having a full-time Business Development and marketing person who is involved in the strategic planning process and the implementation of that plan. This person manages the majority of the day-to-day marketing and Business Development efforts for the company and will include senior principals when required. He or she may manage a staff that supports the marketing activities full time. This person might also be responsible for the production of proposals and marketing materials.

Some firms will have a limited staff. Maybe there is only a marketing coordinator who wears many different hats and provides support at the direction of the firm's principals. Many firms have no marketing staff at all and the principals operate as seller-doers. Either way, the information presented here will be of value.

If you are new to marketing and Business Development, keep in mind there is no such thing as mastery of the art. It is a learned process. Many professional services firms will burn through their opening capital trying various marketing strategies in hopes that they will hit on something that works. That is not necessary. When marketing and Business Development are approached correctly you will see results much sooner, it will take less time, and it will be easier.

Do not expect it to come naturally in the beginning. You must first learn the basic principles, many of which are counterintuitive. Whenever we learn a new skill we go through four stages:

1. Unconscious Incompetence—we don't know what we don't know
2. Conscious Incompetence—we become aware of our need to learn
3. Conscious Competence—we know how, but it's not second nature yet
4. Unconscious Competence—we perform the right thing without even thinking about it

Business Development is a learned skill, and just like any other learned skill, effort must be applied a number of times in order to learn. The knowledge needed to market professional services correctly will be learned one step at a time. Once you learn the basic skills, you will gain control—the control to take your business to any level you wish it to go.

Outcome-Focused **Selling**

When classified as a professional services firm you are most likely selling a service to another person or another business. You may sell your services as a consultant or as a technical firm. Your services may be sold to individuals if you are a CPA, attorney, or physician. Generally Business Development for such firms is classified as *outcome-focused* procurement, rather than behavior or activity-focused. In this book we are focused on the outcome-sales process.

While activity-focused sales works best when selling a product or commodity type service such as trash pickup or retail products, we are talking here about *outcome*-focused Business Development, which works best for relationship-driven sales. It is when:

1. *Skills and knowledge influence* the sale.
2. The sale is more *technical* in nature.
3. The credentialed or technical individual has the freedom and autonomy to *affect the close,* or purchase, due to their understanding of the situation.

4. The sale is based on the customer's need to solve a *problem*.
5. The sales process is based on the customer's *trust* of the technical individual stemming from a relationship.
6. A longer sales cycle is typically involved.

Outcome-focused Business Development tends to be more *forward* thinking. People buy from you because they have a problem to be solved or they have an aspiration that requires professional guidance.

The Business Development Process. Develop systems and processes that help to manage your Business Development efforts or else it becomes an overwhelming exercise that manages you instead. Contacting a potential prospect, setting up an appointment, and establishing a relationship, is a defined process. It's not hit or miss—it's a planned process.

The process is a simple one and should be taken one step at a time. Each step requires a certain set of skills. We will go into greater detail of each step throughout the book, but the overall process looks like this:

1. Decide where your company's technical strengths are and where the business is for that strength.
2. Name a potential client as a new target and conduct research to learn about the company.
3. Find a way to meet the decision-maker—possibly at a networking event or as a referral.
4. Initiate a first meeting to introduce your company, and to learn about the prospect's company and explore needs. It's possible to have made six to nine contacts with the prospect before reaching this stage.
5. Plan the meeting. Gather information by asking the right open-ended questions to uncover new project opportunities and to show how the potential client would benefit from engaging your services.

6. Write a proposal on a project that has been identified to fit your skill set and capabilities.

7. Respond to a short-list invitation from the prospect, or follow up on proposal efforts.

8. Once the prospect becomes an existing client, the process starts again as you work to expand the services you offer to this client.

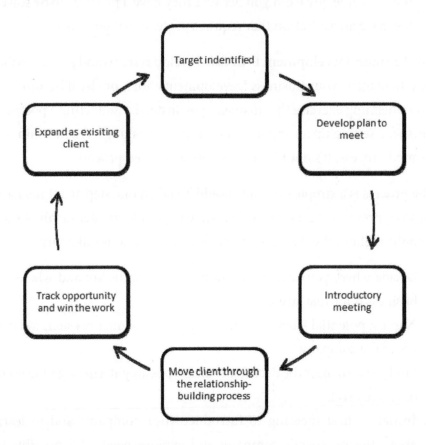

Basically, that's it! As you can see, the *outcome*-focused Business Development process can be lengthy—six or more steps. It all depends on where you enter the process and if you are connecting with the true decision-maker. It can take longer. If it turns out the person you start with is not the true decision-maker, you may have to start the process over again. There may be additional steps, or some steps may be combined, depending on how services are procured and where the buyer is in the process. Working each step as completely and as thoroughly as possible will assure you of developing a strong relationship with the prospective client and having a greater probability of winning future work.

Now, let's go into more detail.

I

THE BASIC PRINCIPLES OF BUSINESS DEVELOPMENT

In this first chapter, the basic concepts of Business Development for a professional services firm will be introduced. Each concept will be further expanded in the following chapters.

It's Not *Magic*! Contrary to popular belief—or wishful thinking—Business Development is not *magic!* It is a learned skill and a step-by-step process. With the right skills and knowledge, anyone is capable. Selling professional services requires focus, passion, and the ability to get out there and hustle! There may occasionally be opportunities that come in the door as referrals, but generally you will not see enough of those to sustain the business. It requires a proactive focus on developing new business opportunities.

Business Development for professional services is an intangible. You must convince people to purchase something they cannot see, yet know they need. The sales process is very different than it would be if you were selling a widget or product. You must first develop the trust of your buyers in order for them to feel comfortable believing that you will give them what they are paying for. For the professional services firm, Business Development is *relationship* driven.

Business Development works best when conducted as a team effort. Everyone in the company has a role to fill, and will hold each other accountable for filling their own roles. Business Development must be made a top priority in the day to day operation of the company. If not, then something else will always come along to interfere and eat up the time. By consistently setting aside just a few minutes each day to focus on Business Development, the technical person selling professional services will see a huge difference in backlog.

Everyone recognizes that in order to be profitable, technical professionals must remain billable in most professional services firms. The problem is that if you allow project work to consume all of your time, then when that job is complete you will have downtime until the next job comes along. It becomes a roller coaster. One must evaluate how that averages out over the course of a year. No matter how much project responsibility you have, it is best to spend small amounts of time on Business Development each day. Be realistic and set your goals accordingly.

It's a Contact Sport. Developing new leads is nearly always going to be done in person if you are in a professional service business. You may occasionally get a lead from your website, but developing new long-term client opportunities will always be a contact sport. To be effective at Business Development, you must be enthusiastic and have the right attitude about the process and enjoy the activities surrounding creating new business opportunities. It can be great fun and very gratifying.

If it does not come easy for you right now, relax; it will become easier as you push yourself and become more experienced. If you want your business to grow, there must be a steady focus and a continuous effort on finding new business opportunities. Attitude is *everything* in Business Development! Never allow yourself or anyone else to feed you negative thoughts or discourage you from your focus and goals.

It is difficult to be effective at developing new business opportunities without enjoying people and being around them, so it is necessary to find ways to do that. It helps to view Business Development as a game. It's an exercise in fitting together several pieces of a puzzle in order to sell the work that you and your colleagues do so well. Become your firm's leader in creating an environment where the entire company focuses on a process for finding new opportunities. Make sure each individual understands his or her role in helping to drive that process. Everyone involved will reap the rewards of a successful Business Development program.

Marketing vs. Business Development. What's the difference between marketing and Business Development? In a small company, most professionals are probably required to do some of both. A carefully crafted combination of marketing activity and Business Development effort is vital for successful business growth when resources are limited.

Generally speaking, marketing encompasses materials and programs designed to reach and persuade potential buyers with websites, media management, and brochures. Those involved in marketing may also manage presentation materials, public relations, direct mail, advertising, and social media in general. Marketing typically assists with the production of a Statement of Qualifications (SOQ) and proposal efforts. An oversimplification is to say that marketing paves the way for Business Development, or is the "paper" part of the sales process.

Business Development, on the other hand, is the people interaction part of sales—the one-on-one personal interactions with prospects and clients. It is the phone calls, meetings, presentations, and networking activities. Both marketing and Business Development must work together seamlessly to accomplish the company's strategic goals.

Everybody Is Part of the Team. Business Development is usually a key activity for the business owner, the Business Development person, and for senior technical professionals, but actually *everybody* in the firm is responsible for creating revenue for the company—either as frontline or as key support team members. Accounting and legal staff should also be considered part of the Business Development team. They must understand the impact they have on the client relationship. Many a good client has been lost because of invoicing or contractual errors or due to the lack of response to client needs.

Frontline Contact and First Impression. The way the office phone is answered can make, or break, a potential client's perception of quality and trust for the company. Business Development should be every employee's responsibility in some capacity. A company can have brilliant people, extraordinary management, and innovative technologies, but all those great things mean nothing if you are not able to reach and talk to the perfect client. The project work is not going to be there unless everyone is communicating effectively with your target clients.

As wonderful as your company may be, the reason for its existence is to make money. In order to make money, you must attract and cultivate quality clients. It's very important to retain and expand existing clients, but statistics show that unless you gain 20 percent of your revenue from *new* clients each year, you are actually losing ground. Ground will be lost due to inflation, client attrition, job completions, and many other factors.

Everything in business begins with sales, and nothing happens until something is sold. Growth is all about bringing in new work and keeping existing clients happy. What we do today will create the project opportunities that are available for tomorrow. It takes commitment and focus.

Don't expect immediate results. Depending on the type of work your company does, some potential clients may take a year or two to develop.

Landing the large projects generally requires more time than landing small short-term projects. Be patient. Remain focused on your goals, and dedicate a small, yet consistent, amount of time each day to Business Development. Today's actions create tomorrow's momentum.

Finding New Business Development Opportunities

There are a number of ways to find new business opportunities and they will vary depending on your type of business. The following are methods to obtain new business that tend to be universal for professional services.

Existing Clients. Keep your eyes and ears open for ways to expand services with existing clients at all times—particularly while you are on the job. Listen to what the client is saying about future plans and make a note to follow up. You may want to involve a senior person or someone assigned to Business Development. Solicit help from your team to follow up on the opportunity; don't try to do it alone. The more people involved, the more likely it is that you will be successful in winning the project. Involving others will usually result in capturing larger projects and will create internal camaraderie among team members.

Referrals. Talk to existing and past clients periodically. Ask about new projects and ask for referrals. You might start by making a list of current clients that you have a good relationship with and discussing possible future opportunities. As you ask for their referrals, you can ask, "Who else should we be talking to?" Or, "Who else would you suggest that we meet?"

Networking. Interaction via networking is a great way to meet people that you might otherwise have trouble getting in to see. Attending a networking event is an excellent way to meet new people, especially if the sponsoring organization is one that your target client attends. Decide on at least one networking organization to join and get involved by working on a committee or volunteering your time. Talk to people about what you do and ask people what they do.

The Elevator Speech. Do you have your elevator speech memorized? The elevator speech can be described like this: If you are in an elevator on the tenth floor and someone asks you what your company does or what you do, can you answer by the time you reach the ground floor?

Try writing out your elevator speech and then memorizing it until you are comfortable saying it and can apply it to various situations. For instance, you will give a different response to someone at a technical event or at a tradeshow or even to a seatmate on a plane, than you would to your next-door neighbor.

Your speech might be about 10 seconds long and go something like this: "I work for _____; we provide _____ services…making sure our clients have a quality, cost-efficient project upon completion" as you continue to explain the *benefits*. Everyone has their own style, but basically you will want to answer the following questions: Who are you? What do you do? What is the *benefit* to your client? Think of it as the reason that you are in business. Customize your elevator speech so that it is relevant to the audience.

When you have the opportunity to speak with a potential client, it's important to sell all the services that the entire company provides, not just what you do. Avoid the "I" word and use "we" whenever possible. It creates the perception of a bigger company and gives the prospect confidence in your ability to provide a depth of resources.

Ideas to Keep in Mind When Contacting New Prospective Clients

Provide Value. Know how you can provide value before you ever make contact. Prospects want to hear how their lives will be enriched or how their job will be made easier by working with you. No one wants to hear about your capabilities or your company history before they understand why they should care. Show the value they will receive from speaking with you now. Eventually, you will sell the company, but first you must sell the idea of meeting with you by letting them know that their time will be well spent by talking with you.

The ultimate offer might be a particular type of assessment you know they need, or an operations evaluation, or another idea you may have. A request for their time must be constructed with great care and polite respect.

High Integrity Approach. As a respectable person representing a quality organization, you have no need to use tricks or to bend the truth, or even to cut corners in order to get their attention. Avoid tactics that you would not want someone to use on you and avoid tactics that you would not want someone to use when talking to your elderly parent. At the end of the day, you must feel proud to tell those close to you about your actions. It's always best to be open and honest. If the only way you can get an audience is to be deceitful, then you are in the wrong business.

It Takes Time. Much more time will be required than most people allow to get to the right person. You must reach the true decision-maker in order to make something happen. Review the company website, news releases, etc. before calling. Expect that you will need to try many times before reaching your target and before any projects come your way. Experience proves that it can often take six to nine times to reach the right person. That number will vary depending on the industry type and the management level you are targeting. The trick is to not give up too soon and learn to make contact without becoming viewed as a pest.

Busywork or Meaningful Business Development Effort. One way to save valuable time is to avoid the busywork—it's a time waster. Some people get so impressed with their "busy-ness" that they fail to recognize that it is much more important to work smarter than to be busy. That particularly applies to Business Development activities. You may feel that you are being productive, but busywork seldom produces the desired results. Spend your time on those activities that will produce meaningful results.

What do we mean by "busywork"? Busywork is spending too much time on the administrative tasks that can relate to Business Development such as research, or writing letters and e-mails and spending hours perfecting them—then getting discouraged when it doesn't work. In addition, handing out brochures or sending out packages of information when there is not a clear reason makes you feel you are doing something, but is not likely to produce the results you want.

There is a time when you need to do research and send out packages and e-mails. However, set a time limit on research and only send brochures and e-mails as part of a defined process for making contact with prospects or to follow up. Don't bombard them with long e-mails and large attachments, or you may irritate and alienate them.

Keep in mind that there is no replacement for getting in front of the right people face-to-face. Having a meaningful conversation designed to find out how you can be of service to them is the *only* way to establish long-term relationships and to gain new project opportunities. Talking to people should be the primary focus for your Business Development activities. Stay focused on the desired end results.

Start with a Plan

In order to make the most of the time spent on Business Development activities, take the time to complete a good plan. A plan that is workable will save you time in the future and will help to avoid frustration that comes with a hit or miss (shotgun) approach to the Business Development process.

Industry Market Sectors. Based on your company's previous experience or expected growth areas, think about industry sectors where you will target your Business Development efforts. Think about projects that have been successful and profitable in the past. It is generally best to focus on no more than six different industry sectors a year; fewer might be better if your company is small. Depending on your business offerings, your industry market sector choices may include retail, education, transportation, energy, health care, developers, contractors, attorneys, and so forth.

Target Clients in Each Sector. Once you have determined what the perfect client looks like for the types of services your company provides, look at your sectors and name those prospects in each that you feel would make good clients. They become your defined targets. Find ways to meet them. Try to stay focused on a set number (maybe ten or twelve) of ideal prospects in each sector within your geographic reach until you have had meetings with them and identified any new business opportunities. If you determine there is no opportunity there, then you can replace the target prospect with a new prospective target.

Learn all you can about your chosen sectors, your targets, and their needs. Attend networking events where your targets will be attending. Follow trade journals, social media, and other resources to stay current on the latest information related to their industries.

Make Contact. Making the initial contact is a very important part of the Business Development process. Research the company and find the right person to speak with, or try to find a mutual contact that will introduce you.

Before you talk with a prospect, either in person or on the phone, plan your discussion as much as possible. Develop open-ended questions to gain the information you need about their potential needs. Understand what they value, and determine in advance the benefits they would gain by knowing about your company's capabilities.

Your next task is to set up a face-to-face meeting. There is no substitute for the face-to-face conversation. You can read body language and see facial expressions, which will tell you so much more than words. The potential client will be more open with information when speaking in person than he or she would be if talking on the phone. Choosing the best form of communication for the first contact will depend on the type of prospect and the urgency of the need to get in the door. If you know they have a project coming up, you should be more assertive.

Try to get someone to refer you and make an introduction. This can be difficult because people are often busy and focused on their respective challenges but if you've helped them out in the past or have a good relationship, most people are willing to make the effort to help you.

You may have to initiate contact with the identified person on your own, which involves a much longer process. If getting an introduction doesn't work out, ask your contact if you can use his or her name when you call the prospect. You might say something like this to the prospective client: "Hello, my name is Sally, and John Doe over at XYZ gave me your name and suggested that I call you. I'm interested in learning more about..."

Manage the Information. Enter all information you have gathered about this prospective client, from research and meetings into an information management system as you go along. A number of different Client Resource Management (CRM) systems exist and your choice will depend on your company's needs.

Follow-Up. After each step in the process, schedule your next action and continue to follow up as long as it takes. Ask your prospect how often they would suggest you call. That way they are giving you permission to make contact again.

Pay Attention to Your Self-Talk. Many people dread the first contact with a new target, either in person or on the phone. Usually the primary reason people want to avoid initiating Business Development calls is fear of rejection. One of the best ways to overcome this fear is to manage your self-talk. The mind is very powerful, and it is estimated that 95 percent of how we feel about something is based on our inner dialogue or the way we talk to ourselves. To control inner dialogue:

- Focus on what you *want* to have happen and worry less about what *might* happen.
- Be confident—you are offering a solution to their problem.
- Remind yourself that they need what you have to offer—they just may not realize it yet.
- They will appreciate your persistence someday.
- Picture yourself helping a friend—most people are better at this than they think.

Networking. The easiest way to meet someone for the first time is at an informal networking function. People are more receptive and tend to be more willing to take the time to meet and visit at these functions and will generally be impressed with someone who wants to meet them. Be upbeat, direct, and professional in your conversation, and remember to avoid monopolizing a person's time. If you want to talk more, try to arrange a time to meet with them later.

Telephone. The most difficult way to make the first contact is on the telephone but sometimes you have no other choice. On the first call you can expect to get voice mail, so plan to leave a message. Clearly state your name and company and the purpose of your call, repeating your name and phone number twice. Speak slowly and deliberately. If the listener does not understand your message the first time, he or she may not bother listening again.

Call two times a few days apart. If you get no results, send an e-mail, but call and leave a message that you are sending it so that the contact is less likely to delete it. Call again in a few days and if there is still no response, leave it alone for a while. Put it on your schedule to try again next month and repeat the process. Sometimes people are busy or out of town but may be receptive to your call another day.

If you do reach the prospect, always be respectful of the individual's time. Ask if you are calling at a good time and if he or she has a few minutes to talk. If the prospect is busy, ask when a better time to call would be. Prospects will appreciate the respect you show for their time. Be able to show how returning your call will be of value to them.

If you know of a project coming up that is a good fit for your company's services, you must be respectfully assertive. Chances are the prospective client will one day thank you for being persistent! The person you have called may not be calling you back because he or she is not the right person, or the person may be on vacation, or may be very busy. Don't give up too soon. Remember, most of the time it will take six to nine contacts before anything happens, and many people give up too soon. Don't give up if it's important that you reach them. Telephone work can be challenging, but it is so important in the Business Development process. There is an entire chapter (chapter 7) dedicated to helping you learn to use telephone skills as another Business Development tool that can work for you.

Voice Mail. A message can work great as a first contact, and is an opportunity to leave an introductory "commercial." Keep this message short. Give them the benefits of working with your firm. Consider giving your name and number at the end of the message and repeating it twice. The reason to do it at the end is that they may listen to the entire message to see who is calling before hitting the delete button.

E-mails. These can be good as a second interaction or as a follow-up, but ask permission first if using it for follow-up or with existing clients. E-mails give you time to compose your message carefully and allow you to attach useful information. Call and leave a message letting them know to look for your e-mail so that they do not delete it without opening it. Avoid words in the subject line that might kick the e-mail to the spam folder. E-mail counts as another of the six to nine contacts it takes to move a relationship along and to uncover an opportunity.

Texting is generally not recommended for the first contact as it can be viewed as more invasive.

Cold or Unannounced Visits. These are not recommended for the professional Business Developer, but may be used as a last resort when you are unable to determine who you need to meet. Unannounced visits are considered to be unprofessional, but many people still do drop in unannounced. An unannounced visit might be an opportunity to establish rapport with the "gatekeeper" or the receptionist, and to set up an appointment to come back later.

One Step at a Time

Keep in mind that successful Business Development is accomplished one step at a time. You have decided that this company might be a good prospect; you've found the right person and will now begin the process of meeting them and establishing rapport.

The First Call. Making the first call is usually somewhat intimidating to most people, so the more preparation you can do, the more comfortable you will feel. The call really does not need to be very long, but just enough to establish credibility. Your goal is to introduce yourself and set up a meeting so that you can learn about them. It is usually best not to talk too long, because the more information they obtain from you at this point, the less inclined they will be to meet with you in person.

Plan before you pick up the phone:

1. Know the objective of the call—what do you want to accomplish? Answer: You want to arrange a meeting to gather information.
2. It is important to be respectful and polite, but not tentative. You want to be strong and confident. The person needs you—but just doesn't know it yet!
3. Be able to articulate how your company can be of service. You've done your research, so you can impart information of value to the prospect. Say something like, "I would like to meet with you to discuss how we can be of benefit to you and your company on the XYZ project".
4. Create a sense of urgency. You might want to let the person know that you plan to be in the area for a specific time and would like to meet briefly while you are there.
5. Keep introductory conversations short. If you give too much information in the first conversation, there is no reason for the person to agree to a meeting. Your goal at this point is to get a meeting set up.
6. Keep the call to less than five minutes. Save any in-depth conversation for the meeting. You just want to get the person's curiosity up at this point so he or she will agree to set the appointment.

The First Meeting. The first meeting you have with a prospective client is such an important time. Too many people go in and try to wing it—that is a mistake. These days, it is so easy to prepare and have a specific plan for the meeting. Taking a little time to prepare can really make a big difference in how the prospective client views you and the outcome of the meeting. Make yourself a checklist of things to do before you meet with the prospect. Make sure you have a plan for the first meeting—to just wing it is a waste of everybody's time.

It's so easy to search online for information about the company and the individual that will provide enough information to allow you to ask intelligent open-ended questions. Check for news articles that have been published in different places. Review the company's website. Read messages from the CEO, any blogs or news releases, and the annual report. All can give you a sense of how the company views the bigger picture and their priorities and future goals. Find out who the people are in the organization that would buy your services, and research them on LinkedIn or Facebook to get an idea of their personal history and background. You can find out where they worked previously, where they went to college, and their interests and hobbies. You may have common interests. By spending a little time up front on research you will have meaningful information that helps you have a more successful first conversation and meeting. Apply research you've done to help build rapport by finding a common interest and guiding the conversation. Prepare to get them talking by using open-ended questions, and then actively listen. Do not interrupt them, because you can learn much more by listening than you can by talking.

As mentioned previously, when you return to the office, be sure to record and store the information you have gathered in your CRM system. You'll be surprised what tidbits of information might prove to be helpful at some point in the future for winning that big project. You are always listening for the client's concerns and issues and if not recorded, they may be forgotten.

Immediately follow up on any action items that were identified. Follow-up is the one step that can make all the difference in moving a prospect through the steps required to becoming a long-term client. It proves that you listened, and will help you gain their trust and respect.

A Call to Action. Here is your action list to get your Business Development efforts started—enjoy the process!

1. Make a list of all existing and past clients that you want to contact.
2. Prepare a list of networking organizations in your area and assign people to attend.
3. Write and memorize your elevator speech. It doesn't have to be anything elaborate, but just something basic that you can memorize and say easily. You will tailor it for each situation.
4. Determine the best market sectors that fit your business.
5. Define the ideal client based on the skill sets in your office, and clients that have been good to work with and have been profitable. Develop a target list based on what the ideal client looks like for your office.
6. Determine your geographic reach. How far from your office do you want to travel to service clients?
7. List information that you want to gather about a particular potential client or opportunity and then form at least five open-ended questions around that.
8. Avoid busywork—stay focused on results!

We will cover all of these points in more detail as we go along. The challenge is in the consistent physical effort of applying the knowledge you gain. It is common for people to spend more time fretting over doing Business Development, or coming up with excuses about why they don't have the time, than just doing it. You can know all there is to know about the Business Development process or your prospects, but if you never get around to contacting them, what good is it? It's like exercise; just get your shoes on and GO!

Key Concepts in this Chapter

1. This chapter is an overview of the Business Development process; details will follow in subsequent chapters.
2. It's not magic! It's a step-by step-process.
3. Identify potential clients for the type of service your firm provides and make a plan for how to reach them.
4. We touched on the various methods of making the first contact with your prospects.
5. Business Development must be thought of as an "Action Process" because without action nothing is going to happen.

2

BECOMING A RAINMAKER

The definition of a rainmaker is one who creates the action or process of producing new business opportunities in the company. It is the creation of a lead for a new project opportunity. A lead is defined as an indication or a clue, about a need or upcoming opportunity. It's up to us as rainmakers to take that lead farther and push it through the Business Development process.

Many people use the terms rainmaker and business developer interchangeably and that can be true. To be a rainmaker or Business Developer is an abstract art, and everybody has their own method according to their personality and comfort level. The skills required for becoming a great rainmaker can be acquired and are learned skills. People are not born with the necessary skills. The good news is that anyone can become a great rainmaker; however, it does require a long-term commitment and continuous learning. Your success, and how well you will develop new leads, depends on several things that can be learned. It is determined by how well you can:

- meet new people
- build relationships
- present to be heard
- write your intentions

- organize activities
- connect with another human being

In order to develop new leads, it is not necessary to telephone strangers and try to sell them something; it's much easier than that for professional services. There are a number of effective things you can do to connect with the people that could potentially give you work.

Historically the rainmakers for professional services firms have been a few senior people, but the scenario is changing as competition increases and as many baby boomers begin to retire. It is not possible for a few people to bring in enough work to feed the entire organization, so it becomes imperative to train younger professionals to fill that void. There is a new generation of rainmakers to be developed.

Every good rainmaker or business developer has a certain mind-set and dedication to a system. The process for meeting people and developing relationships with them will drive that system. Developing your own system is the key to becoming successful. Good rainmakers will have a written plan for their own efforts so that the specific time they have set aside each day will be used for making contacts instead of trying to decide what to do. They will have goals and quotas that they have set for themselves and will track the information gathered so that they can follow up. They will eventually identify new business opportunities from working those leads. Good rainmakers will be assertive and will find ways to meet and interact with lots of new people.

People who consistently exhibit rainmaker principles will achieve the most success. If you intend to be a rainmaker for your firm, the following are the primary habits to cultivate.

1. Rainmakers respect, and always try to satisfy, the best interests of prospects and their clients.
2. Rainmakers are extremely dedicated to becoming top performers—exhibiting the hustle, passion, and intensity it takes to achieve. They are fanatics at goal-setting and following. Goals are a part of their daily routines.
3. Rainmakers just do it because they realize that goals without actions don't get them very far. They know that good intentions are not enough.
4. Rainmakers are masters of market knowledge, customer needs, services their firms offer, their value to the client, their competition, and everything else they need to know to succeed.
5. Rainmakers might not be technical experts in every area, but they know what they need to know in order to promote the services their firms sell.
6. Rainmakers always feed the front of their pipelines, and improve their pipeline quality by having conversations with existing and potential new customers every working day.
7. Rainmakers know how to lead effective Business Development presentations by using needs-discovery questioning and working toward a close of the opportunity.
8. Rainmakers make recommendations and assist their clients and prospects. They become change agents who are not afraid to push when it will be in the best interest of the client.
9. Rainmakers not only conquer their fears, they seek actively to win the most fruitful opportunities no matter how difficult the challenges may be.
10. Rainmakers are constantly striving to learn new skills, and grow and change for the better.

These truths are how successful rainmakers think. Everyone will develop their own style and method of rainmaking, but you must challenge yourself each year to take on more Business Development activity and to be more visible.

We all have different personality types and comfort levels when it comes to rainmaking. Fortunately, there are many ways of generating leads other than making direct calls to people. Consider the many different options to choose from when it comes to lead-generating opportunities. You might become an expert at one or a combination of the following:

- Writing blogs for the company website to share technical information
- Writing articles for trade publications or your company newsletter
- Presenting a white paper at a conference on a technical subject of interest to the attendees
- Speaking at professional association meetings
- Networking with peers or prospective clients
- Attending social events that offer opportunities to interact with potential clients, or to meet people that have the connections to introduce you to prospective clients
- Working tradeshows that offer opportunities to interact with people that you may want to know
- Making educational presentations to groups
- Expanding your proposal-writing skills

Pick a service area or particular discipline area where you feel comfortable, and become a recognized expert on that subject.

Tradeshows. Some rainmakers are great at working tradeshows, which is a special skill. Many people think tradeshows are all fun and games, but if done correctly they are very hard work, both mentally and physically. Tradeshow success is difficult to measure, and participation is about more than just obtaining leads. It is about getting the company name out, shaking hands with prospective clients, learning about them, and telling people about your services. Many times at a show you have the opportunity to explain your services to a new prospect for the very first time and how your company can benefit their upcoming project.

Working a tradeshow can be a very powerful opportunity if done correctly.

Before attending the tradeshow, obtain a list of people that have registered to attend. From the list, choose several prospects that you want to meet, and some that you may have met before but want to talk to again. How many you choose will depend on the length of the tradeshow, but generally spending quality time with five new targeted prospects a day is reasonable. Have a schedule for booth time so that you are not spending all your time standing in the booth waiting for people to come to you. You can also go out and find them. You might attend a session, a luncheon, dinner, or attend an evening event. Keep in mind that at some tradeshows, there are prospective clients who never enter the exhibit hall so go where they might be.

When you meet someone at a tradeshow, you have just begun the process. When you return to the office, follow up with an e-mail and attach a company overview sheet—or a small introduction package regarding the topic you discussed with them. Let them know you enjoyed meeting them and would like to set up a future meeting, especially if you've learned that they have a project coming up. Maybe you could meet for lunch or for a sporting event such as golf.

Never send introduction packages to people that would not welcome the information or send them out to so many people that you can't follow up right away. We all receive information that we just toss and it creates a negative impression, but if you feel that you made a strong connection at the tradeshow, send information and follow up with a phone call. You will stick out in the crowd. And after all, isn't that what Business Development really is all about? Being the one that stands above the rest? At the very least, send a note and keep them on your schedule for periodic follow-up with some piece of information of interest to them. This is the part of your actions that you *can* measure, so keep track of them.

Assist with Indirect Marketing

Rainmakers are great at helping with indirect marketing efforts which help to open the door for Business Development. Writing blogs, e-mails, letters, articles for newsletters, brochures, white papers, and press releases are some good examples of indirect marketing methods. But keep in mind that these methods are just the starting point. Most indirect methods work best if combined with more direct methods of interfacing with prospective clients. You still need to make personal contact and conduct many follow-ups with prospects in order to obtain new business opportunities.

Publishing. Rainmakers are prolific writers and there are many opportunities to use such talents for indirect marketing. The beauty of writing and publishing an article is that you are instantly perceived as an expert. It works best to become an expert in a certain area and write a number of articles about that particular subject. Your article doesn't have to be completed all at once; you can work on it a few paragraphs at a time. Set up a writing schedule that fits into your work schedule.

The process of writing an article begins with an idea. Start writing with the idea of completing work on a page or two, and build from there. Most trade journals want eight to ten pages on a given subject, but check with the journal you want to publish in and ask about their procedure.

Having a specific audience in mind is important in order to stay focused. Write from a particular angle: either agreeable or not, about a new regulation or offer a different perspective about an often discussed technical approach. Tell them what *they* need to know, rather than how much *you* know. They're not interested in everything you know, only in what you know that might benefit them.

Newsletters. Writing for your company's external newsletter is good because it will consistently keep your company's name in front of existing and potential clients. It is very important that newsletters are high quality in both content and appearance, and they must be published consistently. A good newsletter can be used to pull people to your web site and to help establish credibility for your firm's capabilities.

White Papers. A white paper is a report written about a topic of interest that may be presented to an audience. The information is effective in establishing credibility and is nearly always appreciated by the audience.

Blogs. Writing blogs can strongly enhance professional credibility, and is something any level of technical professional can do. They can be written with the idea of posting them on the company website or as an e-mailing to existing or prospective clients. The subject is generally specific and aimed at a targeted group that has a specific interest. Solid rich content ensures that electronic marketing efforts draw attention and ultimately client interest.

Press Releases. Consider writing press releases about projects that your company has completed, or awards and other recognition that your company has received. You might write a release about a team member's accomplishment, such as an innovative approach to an old problem. Deliver your articles to the editors of newspapers or industry trade publications. If you're writing about a project, involve the client and promote the project through the appropriate trade organizations. Be sure to sign your article and provide information regarding where you can be contacted.

Handwrite Personal Notes. Personal notes and letters are rare these days and are more likely to be read than anything else you might send. They can be tailored to the specific objective, and can also be combined with other materials. A good idea is to hand-address the envelope so that it is more likely to get opened and read.

Proposals. Some people have the coveted skill of writing great proposals that sell. A proposal is primarily a marketing document that addresses a prospective client's stated needs which they publish as an RFP (Request for Proposal). A good proposal is one that shows an understanding of the project and proves to the client that you are focused on addressing their needs with the services and experience your company can provide. A good proposal continually points out the benefit of using your company's expertise. Hand-delivering the proposal is ideal. You may not always get to meet the decision-maker, but it makes a good impression that you are prepared to go the extra mile and shows that the client is important to you. When a decision has been made, always follow up in person. Thank the client if you win the bid or ask for a debrief meeting if you do not win. Most companies or agencies are happy to provide such feedback. In the debrief meeting, make sure they understand that you want to work for them in the future and ask how to make that happen the next time.

Public Speaking. Rainmakers learn to enjoy public speaking. Would public speaking be a good Business Development tool for you? As technical professionals we all have unique perspectives and knowledge that can be shared. If you are good at it and enjoy it, by all means find opportunities to speak. If you are not so good at it—you can learn. It's not that difficult and the more you do it, the easier it gets. You might find opportunities at tradeshows, networking events, organization meetings, chamber meetings, or groups of your peers. It generally works best to come from the perspective of educating the audience instead of trying to sell your company. Speaking at just one event each quarter can greatly enhance the visibility and reach of your firm.

The more audiences that you can identify that might have an interest in your message, the more likely public speaking will work for you. Speaking at trade organizations and conferences is a good place to start and can be very powerful. You are perceived as the expert, and people seek you out to talk with and to obtain your opinion on problems or projects. It gains name recognition for the company and puts you face-to-face with your target audience. You may want to ask a client to join you in the presentation if you are presenting information about one of their projects.

Speaking also gives you an opportunity to network before and after the meeting. It's a great way to build your reputation and to generate leads, because your target audiences will self-select when your topic is of interest to them. When speaking at tradeshow, attend the entire event so that you can be accessible to those that are interested in meeting you. Make every effort to be approachable.

Write your own introduction, which should explain why you are qualified to be speaking. As you begin to speak, make a show of turning off your cell phone just before you begin and others will get the hint. Let the audience know how long you'll be speaking and why they should be involved. Don't speak too long…anything over an hour and you lose people. Avoid the details; prepare a handout for the details and distribute it at the end of your talk unless it is necessary for reference during your talk.

Know your audience well enough to be able to tell them what *they* want to know. It is not about what *you* know. Educate them on timely issues and trends and help them understand what it means for them. Ask questions of people in the audience, and if possible call them by name. Others will pay more attention and be more alert if they think they may be called on. Speak clearly in a conversational manner rather than formal phrases. Rehearse a lot so that you feel more at ease and confident. When you are well prepared, giving a speech is not nearly as intimidating as some might think. Practice a lot and make it as interesting as possible to your audience. Ask for feedback from family and friends. Remember, that which we persist in doing becomes easier with time and practice. We will cover presentation skills in a later chapter.

Speaking "On the Spot"

When you are called upon to speak on the spot, it is sometimes difficult to present thoughts succinctly without using filler words, or rambling, to find the point you want to make. First of all, make sure you understand what is being asked for, and then try using *pre-formed lead-in statements* such as:

1. I have something to say about that…(the topic under discussion)
2. The way I see it…(state your point of view)
3. The reason I say that is…(back up your statement with evidence)
4. So, that is why I say…(state your recommendation)

Then wrap it up and sit down. You'll look brilliant, articulate, and well versed on whatever subject is under discussion!

Another scripted way of handling impromptu speaking is the IPES method which stands for: Issue, Position, Evidence, and Solution.

1. State the *issue* as you see it.
2. State your *position* on the issue or problem.
3. Present *evidence* for why you are taking your position.
4. Offer your ideas for a *solution* to the issue.

Either method works for almost any occasion. They work particularly well when talking to prospects or existing clients. Just tie your statements into how you can provide solutions to their stated issues.

Effective Business Development is a Contact Sport

Rainmakers understand that Business Development is a contact sport and they must find ways to come in contact with their prospective client. Fortunately this is not difficult and there are many options available.

Networking. The best way to be a good rainmaker is to network. It is a great way to meet and build long-term relationships with potential prospects. There are two different kinds of networking: one with peers and people that you know, and the other with prospective clients that you do not know yet and will meet at organized functions. Networking with peers and people you already know gains you access to their networks.

Networking at professional association meetings can be time consuming, but can open many doors that would be difficult to open any other way. It's important to participate in the organization in order to be perceived as someone worth knowing. Volunteer for committees and offices; it helps you to gain credibility and visibility. By taking a leadership role, you also improve your own professional abilities and skills. You will be viewed as a peer to be trusted by those that can give you work, and they become more likely to become your advocate. Consider having association meetings at your office. People attending become familiar with your company and others in it.

Working a networking event is an additional skill set to be acquired:

- Arrive early and stay late at a networking event. Before and after the meeting is generally the best time for networking.
- Make an effort to speak to those you already know, but also speak to at least five new people.
- Spend five to ten minutes with each person and then move on. If you want to talk further, set up a lunch meeting. Don't try to sell your services; instead, sell an appointment to talk further.

- Never sit with coworkers. Split up and cover more territory.
- Collect business cards from everyone at your table. People are flattered when you say, "May I get your business card?" It makes them feel important.

Be enthusiastic and enjoy the process. Ralph Waldo Emerson said, "Nothing great was ever achieved without enthusiasm."

Get to know people. How do you know if a person you are meeting for the first time can be a good networking resource for you? Just *ask*. Obtaining answers to just a few questions will help you determine the potential value of networking with this person. You might ask:

"What does your firm do?"

"What is your position?"

"How long have you been with the firm?" (This gives you an idea of the amount of credibility and clout the person carries within his or her firm.)

"What is your target market?"

"Who are your clients?"

The most important of all the rules of networking is to stay in touch and follow up. Becoming a successful networker takes a time commitment, persistence, and patience. You have to be willing to give first. But mastery of the skill of networking will result in you being seen as a leader, and you will bring in more business opportunities for your company.

Educational Seminars or Lunch & Learns. Conducting seminars or training classes can be another great method for gaining credibility for you and for your company. You establish yourself as an expert that is giving back to many people at one time. You don't have to compete for attention, and there is a strong opportunity to develop personal relationships you can build upon.

You can charge a small fee to help cover costs. Actually, a fee is preferable. The perception is that if there is a charge, the event is of more value, and people are more likely to show up if they have paid. If you have a special client you want to make sure attends, you can always offer to comp their lodging or travel costs. It's also a good idea to give them something to take home—maybe a book on the topic. The item must be good quality, or else it is best not to give anything all.

When conducting a seminar, encourage interaction. Have an open space or area where people can stand and talk before and after the presentation. During the networking time, you and others in your firm will play host and make sure everyone feels they are benefiting from being there.

Interact with your attendees and ask, "What is your interest in coming to this event?" Listen for ways to help. If someone asks a question that you cannot easily answer, let the person know that you will follow up with additional information. Do so within the next week. Be sure to obtain business cards and to follow up with every person attending.

Lunch & Learns work great for attorneys, contractors, and engineers to present at client's or prospect's office where there are groups of people that have an interest in the information. Present information from their perspective and explain how it will benefit them in their business. Focus primarily on information related to their industry.

This is the time for an informal presentation because they will be eating. Provide a good quality, easy-to-eat lunch. A recommendation would be to provide a deli sandwich box lunch that contains everything an individual might want. There will be fewer disruptions than there would be if food was provided that required participants to get up for more food items. They can focus on what is being presented rather than think about what they are going to get next. You might want to bring a box of cookies to be left in the break room, or put them in a basket with business card attached and a few brochures tucked inside. It creates conversation within the department about your company and how you could help with projects.

Consider teaming with a complementary firm that targets the same clients that you do when conducting Lunch & Learns. For instance, an engineering firm might team with a law firm to present information on new regulations. There could be some overlap of service offerings, but potential conflicts can be resolved if discussed up front. While it is understood that you are there to sell your services, it generally works best for the sales portion to be understated or not said at all.

Attendees understand that if you are talking about it, you can do it for them. Have flash drives or printed information available that they can take if they are interested. You can always follow up with additional information or provide the presentation electronically with links to reference material.

Seminars, conferences, and special events will remain some of the most powerful tools for marketing professional services, even though they demand more time than many other forms of Business Development. They tend to be complex, expensive, and deadline oriented. There are hundreds of tasks that must be completed on time. But all organizational tasks can be weighed against the enormously extensive benefits.

Internal Brown Bag Seminars. Educational seminars can be conducted internally for staff by those that have a special expertise. It is a way of sharing knowledge with peers so that they can provide the information to their prospective clients as a way of selling the company's total services and capabilities.

Social Situations. Social situations are good ways to come in contact with and to build relationships with existing and potential clients. In social situations, people tend to be more relaxed and receptive to interaction with those that they do not know. At these events it is usually best to keep your interactions light and follow up later to set up meetings to discuss business. This is just a good opportunity to get to know people more personally.

Sporting events such as golf outings are an excellent way to meet and get to know people. Invite existing or prospective new clients to play golf. There are several different theories about discussing business on the golf course. Most people like to concentrate on their game, so wait for the client to take the lead. Generally, at some point they will ask what you or your firm does and then you can give a brief summary of your company services. Save the heavy stuff for later. There really is never a good time to get "salesy" on the golf course. During the social time or after the game, you can ask questions that might help direct the conversation toward new business opportunities.

Any sport or group activity is a good opportunity to network. There are those that prefer tennis, football, or other sporting events, so get to know potential clients well enough to learn what they might enjoy doing and then extend an invitation. Remember that your Business Development efforts must always match the ethics of the game—honesty, good manners, and consideration are always required.

Rainmakers understand that Business Development is a contact sport. They know how important it is to be where people are and to find ways to interact with them. You can do this any way that is comfortable for you—but you must find ways to have meaningful interactions with people if you want to be a productive rainmaker. Social media can be a part of the effort but to be effective Business Development must be conducted face-to-face.

Lead Generation

We hear a lot of talk about lead generation, but seldom do we see much about the details and tactics for generating those good leads that bring in new business. To be a successful rainmaker and professional services prospector—one that is able to fill a pipeline with quality leads—there are a few basic things you must do:

Have a Good Target List. Prospecting success depends on the strength of a quality list of potential clients and your ability to precisely target those that need the services your company provides. Consultants tend to focus too low in the organization when making initial contact and then try to work up from there. It may be easier to get an audience at a lower level because people are more willing to talk with you. However, it is much more productive to start at the top to reach the decision-makers. People at the top can help you reach the decision-makers you need more quickly, and a word from them on your behalf carries more weight. Make sure you have the true decision-maker before you start, or you will waste a lot of time talking to nice people who do not have the ability to help you.

Keep a Healthy Pipeline. One of the problems some rainmakers get into is that they let their pipelines become stale and clogged with useless leads. That is where having a defined perfect client profile is helpful. Maintaining a healthy pipeline is important to closing new business. As more leads are generated we tend to add them to the ones that are already there, and our pipeline becomes clogged with useless leads. Keep it clean by reviewing it often and sifting through to make sure the current leads are worth your time and focus.

Decide which leads are worth nurturing, based on your predefined criteria for the perfect client, and keep those that fit. Discard or put aside those that can eat up your time. Stick to your targeting parameters. Your time is an investment in your business, and if you are spending time tracking useless leads, you are wasting a valuable resource.

Search for RFP (Request for Proposal) postings. Another way of finding leads and new opportunities that are up for bid is through Internet resources. Where you search online depends on your type of business: Fed Biz Op, state procurement sites, trade journals, or other industry-common sites. There are also commercial search subscription services available. When you find an RFP posting, make sure it is for your target market and that the requester knows your company before spending time responding to the RFP. Submitting proposals when there is no existing relationship seldom works and could be considered busywork. Know your criteria for proposals before spending time on them.

Manage Self-Talk. When you are preparing to talk to someone or make a phone call, pay attention to your self-talk and don't allow yourself to be talked out of it! Never second guess what the potential client's reaction is going to be. You really never know.

Provide Value. Know how you can provide value before you ever make the contact. Prospects want to hear how you can enrich their lives by working with you. Nobody wants to hear extensive details about your company capabilities unless you can relate them to their needs. They need to understand why you care about their needs before they will hear you. Show the value of the time they will spend meeting and talking with you first. Remember to always be respectful of their time. As you uncover needs, you can then show the value of your capabilities for specific problems.

Finding the Time. It can be a challenge for technical staff, with utilization responsibilities, to find the time for writing, networking and other lead-generation activities. There are many ways to make efficient use of the time dedicated to Business Development activities. Consider double use of items you have written:

- Use a speech as the base for an article or blog.
- Use the same speech and tailor it to give to different groups from various perspectives.
- Use the same article for multiple publications by giving it a slightly different slant for each.
- Speak at a number of professional association meetings that you plan to attend anyway.
- Use research conducted for another purpose for a speech, a press release, or an article.
- Turn information that you've put together for a training class into a speech or white paper. Use class materials for a speech or white paper.

Communication Tools. Develop your skills and use a variety of methods for making contact. Different people will respond to different communication methods, so you may have to try several before hitting on the right one. Some people respond to phone calls, and others respond to e-mails. Snail mail can be effective, as can fax in some cases. You might try a combination of phone calls and e-mails.

Don't Give Up. Great rainmakers don't give up when they know a target needs their services. Remember, it can take as many as nine times to reach the contact. After nine tries, if there is no success you may want to put the effort on the back burner for now and try again in a few months. You might be more successful if you can meet the decision-maker at a networking event first. Then try the process again.

Becoming a great rainmaker takes a persistent focus of dedication to becoming a top Business Development performer in the company. Stay focused on results, avoid the busywork, and be persistent and success will come.

Track Your Progress

There are many reasons to track progress. It provides milestones, encouragement and motivation, it encourages teamwork and it also helps to make sure no lead falls through the crack to be lost. Tracking progress begins with tracking the Business Development activity of each individual.

The following is an example of a Business Development Activity tracking form that can be used for technical professionals. Make it as simple or as complex as you choose, the purpose is to define what you want staff to focus on for accomplishing Business Development Plan related goals. Make sure activities such as networking events follow the listed goals of the company's plan.

January
Business Development (BD) Report

Name	Title/Dept.	Recommended hours/ week for BD	Actual week 1/07	Activity Description	Actual week 1/14	Activity Description
John Smith	Project Geologist	10	9	NENP 7 TCEC	8	FFMEC – ACME Company
Susan Allen	Staff Engineer	5	8	IBDS 5 TCEC	5	NEP
Mark Jones	Senior Manager	20	24	TS IBB	21	LL, IBDS, FFMFC

Reporting Codes:

- NEP   Networking Event—Peers
- NENP   Networking Event—Non-Peer (to meet prospective clients)
- TCEC   Telephone Calls to Existing Clients for BD purpose
- IBB   Internal Brown Bag Technical Presentation
- LL   Lunch & Learn (for client or potential client)
- PTPEA   Presented Technical Paper to External Audience
- FFMEC   Face-to-Face Meeting with Existing Client for BD purpose
- FFMFC   Face-to-Face Meeting with Future Client for BD purpose
- IBDS   Internal Business Development Seminar/training
- ECRP   Existing Client-Requested Proposal Development
- TS   Tradeshow

Note: Codes available for brevity—use additional description if necessary.

Key Concepts in this Chapter

1. A Rainmaker is a business developer who creates leads and generates new business opportunities for the firm.
2. There are many methods of creating new business leads and meeting prospective clients.
3. Everyone will have different comfort levels, choose one or two methods and become the expert.
4. Rainmakers cultivate certain habits that help them to be successful.
5. Good Rainmakers manage self-talk and push themselves to be more effective.
6. Corporate management must allow for and encourage rainmaker activities.

3

ENTRY-LEVEL PROFESSIONALS: A VALUABLE RESOURCE

With increased competition, it is very difficult for a small firm to generate enough business with just a few senior people focused on Business Development. Young professionals can be a valuable resource for Business Development with just a little training and mentoring. Small changes in the organization's method of procuring new business can lead to a large increase in revenue. Think of it: If everyone in the company feels a responsibility to bring in new business, then your company becomes its own sales engine. It's leveraging what is already there, and the momentum that is created feeds itself. Build a culture in your firm that drives Business Development by making sure everyone is clear on their roles in the process. Young people make great rainmakers because they are energetic, enthusiastic, and resourceful. Capture that and you can open all kinds of doors for new business opportunities.

Small businesses will generally have a larger percentage of young technical professionals. Harness this valuable resource and your company is capable of achieving more than a larger firm with mature staff. As management, your role is to recognize the importance of having every front-line employee able to articulate the firm's differentiators and its benefits and value to the client. Some young professionals may not be front-line employees yet, but they will be someday, so the most valuable thing you can do for them and the company is to begin to train them.

What Is Business Development and Selling? The best way for young technical professionals to become seller-doers is to help them to understand the concept of selling professional services. Selling is not just picking up the phone and making cold calls. It's not just networking at industry events, either. Selling professional services is more than that. It is:

- using any opportunity at your disposal to target the right prospects
- turning a lead into a prospective job
- representing the capabilities and benefits of your firm by doing good work
- keeping others at your firm apprised of potential opportunities
- identifying opportunities to expand and provide additional services to existing clients
- communicating your firm's value proposition to as many prospective new clients as possible
- introducing new capabilities and services that support current and future work

You can buy a product or a vacation package from a nameless person on the phone or online, but that's not how it works when selling professional services. Revenue typically flows through a person in the firm, from a person (client) needing a service.

Young technical professionals are usually eager to help build the business, but they need coaching and mentoring. They have worked hard to complete their technical studies and are now entering the real world of consultancy. They may be a bit shocked at the real-world expectations they now encounter. They can be coached to help round out that technical degree with a few real-world elements that will help to guarantee their professional success. Training opportunities are built into every day. Young people naturally have a proactive desire to grow, however, they may need help learning such things as self-monitoring, client interaction, and conducting performance evaluations.

Young technical professionals must strive to become experts in your company's field, expanding their technical skills and understanding to encompass a wide range of activities related to the kinds of projects and the types of markets you wish to pursue. They need to understand why and how the company makes money.

Expectations and contributions should be:

- customized to an individual's role and where that person is in his or her career, but should cause the individual to stretch a little
- measured and tracked through specific goals that are formed jointly with his or her manager
- tied to the broader Business Development plan of the company
- focused on strengthening existing client relationships and finding ways to meet new prospects

Teach Effective Communication Skills. As young technical professionals are faced with increasingly complex issues on a project, they are responsible for understanding how to communicate those problems to the project manager or directly to the client. You can coach them to anticipate problems even before they arise, and to communicate effectively about those problems. They may need nurturing in communication skills.

Young technical professionals will need to understand how to communicate with clients. Make sure they know how to listen. Expose them to various types of clients and their needs, temperaments, and expectations. As they gain confidence and are trusted by their senior peers, they will grow in the necessary skills. In time, they will have a chance to build rapport and develop relationships directly with clients.

Balance. If you are mentoring young professionals, help them balance and apply new knowledge to helping clients and solving problems. You will want them to stay well rounded and continue to enjoy family and hobbies outside of work. A well-rounded individual is generally happier.

Help them work smarter to ensure that they are clear on the productivity and profitability goals for each assigned project. Help them prepare for the day when they are faced with leadership responsibilities. Some of these might be for staffing requirements or for production in order to keep project performance on track.

Work with young professionals to develop personal plans, not only for their careers but to support the company Business Development efforts. Help them evaluate their strengths and weaknesses to determine where additional training could be of value. They may just need additional exposure or experience in a certain area. Encourage them to share with others. By sharing their plans with others, they will feel more ownership for their own growth plans.

Identify role models and mentors for them and teach them how to work with and value the relationships. Young professionals will be more committed to an organization that values them as people and cares enough about them in the early years of their careers to invest in making a positive impact on their lives. As they gain experience they will respond to greater and greater expectations and responsibilities.

Cross-training with all departments can be very valuable. It helps employees gain an understanding of the workings of the firm, how the departments work together, and how the individual fits. It creates empathy for the responsibilities of others in the organization. If an employee is shy, conducting a technical webinar on a favorite technical issue might be a good starting place.

Teach young technical professionals to offer help to other departments as much as possible, particularly marketing and Business Development. They will learn that everyone is responsible for marketing and there is never enough help with those activities and they are never finished. There is always more that could be done. They will learn better how to recognize new business opportunities and may be less prone to complain that marketing is not doing enough for them. In addition, project managers tend to favor those that show an interest in becoming a part of something more than their own tasks.

Teach young technical professionals that clients are king and doing great work for them is a given—they need to do more than is expected in order to stay ahead of competition. Help them understand that expanding client services and providing extra value is good for business.

For an entry-level professional, technical competence is the bare minimum and is required to keep the job. A primary value that a young professional can bring to the firm is his contribution to the Business Development effort. Learning solid Business Development skills can move a young person further along on his or her career path faster than anything else. Spend time and effort training young professionals to do Business Development and marketing, and they will become valuable resources for the firm. Listed below are skills that can be learned and will add value to the role of young professionals. Teach them to:

1) **Communicate.** Business Development and marketing success comes as a result of good communication and listening skills. Learning how to ask the right questions and listening for opportunities can be most valuable.

2) **Pay attention to detail.** Technical professionals have the ability to understand complex occurrences that have an impact on technical solutions. Marketing applies that same keen attention to detail to almost every phase of the effort. Technical people are generally good at uncovering leads buried within obscure information, and creating materials that are very accurate in content and presentation. Because of their training to observe details, young technical people are great at picking up on hints from a prospective client. Especially when they have been trained on what to watch for during a face-to-face meeting.

3) **Reward and recognize.** Many professionals will find marketing fun when they learn the right things to do to help the firm grow. You may have to help them figure out how to have fun beyond their comfort zones. Show them instances where their input, their cooperation, and their active participation can strengthen the organization's marketing success. Generously reward and recognize them when they succeed.

Networking

Teach young professionals that all employees are expected to sell the services that the firm provides, even though they may do it in different ways. Networking is a career-long focus for professional services, but some young professionals may be fearful of networking. Many will say, "But I am uncomfortable talking to strangers." Teach them methods that can help them become more comfortable talking to strangers. Most technical people are introverts and may not enjoy talking to strangers. Find ways to help them overcome the intimidation.

Teach networking and speaking skills, and teach young professionals to understand the value to the firm of good technical networkers. They may work best with a "buddy" in the early years. They can hold each other accountable, introduce each other, and to enjoy the process more.

Firms that believe a young person should be seasoned before taking on networking responsibilities are missing the boat. Young people are naturally social and you can teach them the rest with a little patience.

The conversation part of networking can be a challenge for some people. They may wish they could just hang around with a few people they know, or just show up and have a drink, listen to the presentation, and then get out of the place as quickly as possible. They may rush to go home or back to the office to work on some very important report. You must stop that line of thinking. Teach them that there is nothing more important than being where you are and doing what you are doing while at a networking event. The trick is to make the best of each networking opportunity while you're there, and then to follow up in order to make something happen.

There is no such thing as someone having a natural "gift of gab." Talking to people is a learned skill, just like anything else. It's not a big mystery and anyone can do it with proper guidance. Instruct young professionals to make an effort and to learn. Educate them on how to start a dialogue, to be interesting, and maybe even be a bit memorable. People attend networking events to meet other people—they are all there for the same purpose. Show them how to just walk up to someone and say, "Hello." Most people will appreciate it.

Networking is not just a socializing event; it can be hard work when done properly. There is something magical about the act of networking; it can provide so many benefits, both personally and for the firm. It is a way to share with peers and to meet and speak with people that would not talk with you otherwise. It's a great way to meet potential new clients. When they have met you at a networking event, they feel that they know you and are more likely to take your calls and to trust you. Because they know you, they are more likely to give you the project when one comes up than they would to someone they do not know.

Networking helps to further existing client relationships, too. It gives you the opportunity to learn about industry trends. As young professionals become involved with the organization, both they and the firm will be perceived as leaders in the industry. It is assumed that they are more knowledgeable than those firms or individuals that are seldom seen. Networking can be an effective tool for the young professional to learn. As with anything else, the more you do it, the easier and more productive you become, and the more fun it becomes!

Orchestrating Success for Anyone. Why do some companies grow and others fail? Why are some people highly successful at Business Development while others struggle to even make a contribution? Is it fate or is it just luck? No, it is a conscious decision.

Young or old, consistently successful people have similar qualities:

- They think about and make choices resulting in the right decisions for their personal lives and their careers. They consciously define what they want to get out of life.
- They develop a strong focus on goals and their missions. They understand that new blasts of daily information tend to erode current knowledge, and historical knowledge can interfere with the understanding of the new information. Keeping personal development ideas top of mind keeps successful people from becoming lost in the overload of new information.
- Successful people design the kind of lives they want, and set aside time each week to work toward that lifestyle.
- Recognizing that all careers are a series of takeoffs and landings, some rough and some smooth, successful people will seize the

opportunity to grow. Many find success by digging deeper where they are, and others may move around to find it.

- Successful people know that becoming consistently persistent is a choice to be made and that having a good life goes far beyond having a good time.
- Practice every day. A lottery ticket can make you a millionaire but it won't make you a successful person. Daily practice is the way to a consistently successful life.

Young professionals should realize that the mind is a powerful tool when it comes to success, but there are just a few steps to obtaining anything you want.

1. Ask consistently—focus on what you want. Spend time giving it thought; be very clear and concise.
2. Expect and believe—add the power of emotion. What does it feel like to have what you want in your life right now?
3. Allow it to happen—expect it to be true. Believe that you will have it. Whenever you feel a negative thought entering your mind, say, "Stop!" and replace the negative thought with a positive thought.

Spend five to ten minutes morning and night focusing on goals and showing appreciation for moving a step closer. Try this exercise for two weeks. Get into a happy secure state—whatever that is for you. Now, focus on envisioning. Talk out loud to yourself and write it down. Feel it in the present tense, as if you already had what you want. Do this for ten minutes every day, and at the end of two weeks you will be amazed at the results and the change in your attitude.

Working with Younger People. We have more generations in the workplace today than ever before in history. Each generation uses a different language. If you are a senior manager, here are a few things to know about generational differences that might prove helpful. Young professionals born after 1980 will:

- Receive and process information differently.
- Love technology and may assume it is the answer to every problem.
- Tend to require frequent short snippets of information rather than long drawn-out lectures.
- Possess a can-do attitude and are highly collaborative and optimistic.
- Want to have a voice and be heard.
- Want a defined career path and a boss who will help them get there with one-on-one mentoring.
- Believe that group meetings are a waste of time so you may have to help them see the value of sharing information, for themselves and for the company.
- Expect a blended social and work life to be the normal and may need support for how best to do that.
- Have a stronger media focus regarding personal branding. They may require mentoring to establish long-term face-to-face relationships.
- Try to do too many things at once and may lose focus on important tasks. Help them identify and maintain priorities.

Working with young people can be a joy when approached with the right attitude. They soak up information so rapidly, and are not afraid of the risk required to apply new ideas.

<u>Key Concepts in this Chapter</u>

1. Small companies have limited resources and so must teach younger professionals how to be effective Business Developers.
2. Teach them effective communication skills and how to interact with prospects and existing clients.

3. Teach them to be comfortable in networking situations that can produce leads.

4. Help them to learn to balance life and work.

5. Working with various age groups can prove challenging so managers must understand how various generations process information.

4

THE BUSINESS DEVELOPMENT PLAN

Any important undertaking requires a plan and a strategy for how goals will be accomplished. A good plan is particularly necessary when it comes to Business Development. Without a plan, you will not be making the most of the time dedicated to growing your business. Strategy is the outline for what you plan to achieve; it keeps your actions on track and focused on those activities that make a difference. You can periodically make adjustments for changes in the environment, but your plan tells you what you will do today, tomorrow, or next quarter in order to get to where you want to be next year or in the next five years.

Create a Business Development plan that is a working dynamic document, aimed squarely at specific results. Then methodically implement the plan. Your Business Development plan will be used as a guidebook for each Business Development effort that you undertake. If an opportunity is presented, it must fit within your plan and the goals that you've laid out, or it will just become a distraction from your overall objective. Distractions will ultimately impede the success of your business.

Tie It to the Corporate Business Plan. Business Development planning is tied to the company's corporate plan, but is more focused on creating opportunities that provide new business and will in turn have an impact on revenue. A good plan will produce greater Business Development results for your efforts because it:

- Provides a road map and sets the guidelines for priorities and targets.
- Keeps the team focused and pointed in the same direction.
- Will ultimately require less time and produce greater results.
- Will take the guesswork out of the process of developing new business opportunities.
- Defines the path forward while applying a systematic approach.
- Helps to budget resources in the right places.
- Establishes accountability and methods of measurement.
- Keeps you from getting caught up in someone else's priorities.
- Keeps everyone clear and focused on what needs to be done next.
- Gives you a point to return to for restarting your Business Development activities if you become sidetracked.

Many small firms make the mistake of thinking that since they are just getting started they will just accept any new work that is offered. They believe there is no reason to go to all the trouble of developing a strategy or plan. They may feel that they are doing just fine and don't have time to focus on planning. This is a big mistake. More than likely, the company is just surviving and will continue to operate in survival mode.

The world is too competitive and changing too rapidly to leave the growth of your business to chance. At some point the business begins to run the owner instead of the owner running the business. When the same amount of effort is focused on specific targets rather than on reacting to events, the company will be stronger and you will have more control over the growth. When you are working from a plan, having your own business can become fun again!

Take the time to clearly define your focus. While it is good to have some flexibility in your plan, it has been proven that the shotgun approach to Business Development, for any sized firm, does not work and is a waste of resources. Create specific objectives and develop a strategy for opening doors and creating new business opportunities. By planning you will be doing less work in a targeted way, which is much more effective.

The Shotgun Approach. This is everybody doing their own thing in order to feel busy. They keep trying various things until something happens. The perception is that they are doing *something* to contribute to the Business Development effort. The problem with this method is that it produces very few results, is frustrating, and is a great time waster—all of which can be very discouraging and not much fun. Business Development should be fun.

The purpose of the Business Development plan is to keep everyone focused on the target and pointed in the same direction. In this way, meaningful efforts will ultimately take less time and produce greater results. The plan helps to set up specific targets in order to avoid the shotgun approach.

Outline the Action. Depending on the type of business you are in, your plan may be different in content and layout, but every good plan will contain similar information. The thing to remember is that Business Development can only be accomplished through *action*. Your plan is a vehicle that helps you to move to action. By creating a targeted plan, you are just mapping out the action part of your Business Development effort.

Parts of the Plan. The basic parts of every good Business Development plan are these:

1. Define guiding statements, or the purpose for your business stated through mission and vision statements—where the business plans to grow. It clarifies what you plan to accomplish.

2. Conduct a SWOT analysis. A SWOT analysis is a picture of your company's **S**trengths and **W**eaknesses, as well as the **O**pportunities and **T**hreats that exist in the marketplace.

3. Identify the best market sectors for your business and the best potential prospects within each sector based on your SWOT analysis. You will also define the perfect client and type of project that is best for your firm's skill sets. This section is important and needs the most detail, and probably will require the most work.

4. Implementation Plan. As you discuss the implementation of your plan, you will determine who is responsible for what and how they will do it, and how each activity is to be measured. Discuss who (the team) and how you will carry out the defined goals. Determine the method of communication and develop a schedule. Determine who will be responsible for each target and how you plan to measure and hold each other accountable.

5. Budget planning is the final step—putting the cost numbers to what you have decided to accomplish.

As we go into more detail, keep in mind that even the most beautifully constructed plan is just a piece of paper unless it is implemented and put into action. Goals and objectives should be tracked and measured, or they are not going to be real and will never work.

Another part of planning is to determine how long it will take and what it will cost, and make a reasonable estimate of the amount of profit to be gained. There is not much sense in putting a lot of time and effort into something that is not going to produce results and profit.

Your plan does not need to be elaborate, but it *does* need to be accessible to everyone that will be involved in the Business Development process. Store the file on a central drive that is easily accessible, because you will want to refer to it often and update your plan quarterly. Then conduct a complete reevaluation annually. Some companies like to see a printed copy on their shelf—that's fine as long as it's in a form that can be changed as often as needed. A loose-leaf binder and lots of white space on each page for notes makes it easy to manage.

Brainstorm. To start building your plan, pull your key employees together and host a brainstorming session. Hold the event off-site away from distractions. Give people plenty of notice so they can prepare and put their thoughts together. A suggested brainstorming session guide is included in the next chapter to help get you started.

Sections of the Business Development Plan

Your Business Development plan can be as elaborate or as simple as you choose—it can be one to fifty pages—but in general it should include the following sections.

Section 1—Purpose, Goals, and Objectives

Define the purpose for your Business Development efforts. Start with: How do you want to be viewed by the world? What is your specific objective? What do you want your efforts to accomplish for the company? What is your revenue goal?

To determine this, think about these questions: What is the current business situation for your company? Are you busy? Great! Now ask yourself, is it the type of work you really want to do? Are you working with the *type of client* that you *want* to work with, or are you putting up with people that do not appreciate the value of your work? Is your focus on long-term growth, or is it a sudden burst of new business that may die off? Evaluate where you've been and where you want to go.

A purpose or vision statement for your plan could involve becoming known to a certain market in a certain length of time, or adding a certain number of new clients this year in a particular market sector.

An objective is defined as an actual end *result*. Determine goals to be achieved within a specific time frame. Outline your strategy for accomplishing your objectives and list the specific activities that will be done to achieve those objectives.

What you want to achieve is a steady flow of work, with the type of clients that you want who have the type of projects that fit your skill set. Or you may want to grow into new market areas. It's not going to happen quickly, so take the time to make your efforts effective by planning and strategizing. You really can be picky about the type of client you want to work with if your Business Development efforts are focused on the right things.

Section 2—The SWOT Analysis

Conduct a SWOT analysis. A SWOT analysis is a great tool for helping set criteria and identifying your strengths and weaknesses, and examining the opportunities and threats you face. Give this activity plenty of time because everything else will be based on this information.

To begin, just make a large table of 4 squares, one block for each of your: strengths, weaknesses, opportunities, and threats (SWOT), and then list what they are for your company. Think about them not from your perspective, but from the perspective of your potential prospects, your competitors, and the general market.

- **Strengths** are the positive characteristics of the business, or the advantage you have over competitors. Strengths tend to be more internal; they are your company's skill set or expertise, previous project experience, or the fact that you are a small company and can be responsive to client needs. Consider the experience of personnel, company reputation, and proximity of office location to the prospective targets. Look at established relationships in a particular market. When listing your company strengths, think about them in relation to your competitors. If you have the same strengths as your competitors, then they are not really considered strengths but necessities, and are expected by your target prospects. Find the strengths that are unique for your firm.

- **Weaknesses** are internal areas of limitation. They are the things that place the team at a disadvantage and that need improvement. Weaknesses might be the lack of a particular skill set or knowledge. They could be personnel resources, experience levels, or lack of market presence or reputation in a particular industry segment. A weakness is any problem or obstacle that might stand in the way— even if the obstruction does not have an obvious solution, such as lack of funding for a particular market sector. It might be a client's perception that a small company cannot handle large projects.

- **Opportunities** are external chances to improve profits, such as improving economic conditions, availability of better qualified new hires, new market trends, areas for growth, or target prospects where you know someone. Look at your strengths and see what opportunities, or areas of growth, they could open up for the firm. Look at weaknesses and see what opportunities might open up if they could be eliminated.

- **Threats** are those external obstacles that must be overcome in order to pursue a chosen target sector. They might include lack of funding, changing technology, a dying industry, lack of knowledge, an unknown company, or competitors gaining ground in your area.

To take it a step further, you can apply the same analysis to what you know about your competition and see where you can gain an advantage. Recording as much information as possible about the competition helps you to understand what you will be up against in the market, and what the potential targeted clients know about each of you. Applying a SWOT analysis before responding to RFPs could clarify the Go/No-Go decision.

Section 3—Targeting

Determine where to focus your efforts by identifying market sectors and the potential prospects in each sector. You will need to decide what areas or sectors to target, such as education, health care, transportation, and so forth. When making sector choices, evaluate potential customer needs, potential for profitability, and potential for long-term growth. Your sector choices should be based on existing or easily obtainable staff expertise in your company.

Look at the risk of focusing on the chosen sectors—sometimes the risk is the trade-off of time. If you spend too much time on a sector where you are unknown it may not be profitable for some time. You could lose the time that might have been spent on more profitable efforts—it's a trade-off. Another trade-off risk is to spend too much time on a sector that will increase your long-term growth at the risk of missing short-term opportunities. It generally works best to keep a balance of short-term and long-term pursuits.

Generate ideas that will help differentiate your business from the competition in your chosen sectors. When deciding on which sectors to target, consider the following:

1. Your company's particular areas of expertise and the available skill sets.
2. Where most of the work is coming from currently.
3. New growth opportunities in the market.
4. The types of companies and projects that make the most sense for the company long term.
5. Prospective clients who have funding for projects that will fit your skill set.
6. Opportunities that are likely to be the most profitable.

Determine a geographic radius for travel that makes sense. It is usually best for a small business to keep a local focus. Most find it more effective to be a big fish in a little pond than to be a little fish in a big pond.

Conduct your own research to help make decisions about sectors and the target clients to pursue. Don't depend on hearsay; others may be relying on old information. While it is sometimes good to accept opinions and input from others, know that they may be repeating the same old information they heard from someone else. It may have been the market last year, but is not necessarily the market this year. Researching on your own for original information puts you ahead of your competition. It helps you be the first into a market. There are a number of ways to research for information: web searches, trade journals, networking groups, trade organizations, and the opinions of those you trust to be up on the latest market information.

Another thing to decide: Do you want to focus on previous clients, current clients, or new clients? Or, do you want a combination of all of these? It seems to be more exciting and glamorous to focus on gaining new clients—it's what we talk about, reward, and recognize. But the truth may be that the best and most immediate opportunities are with previous or existing clients.

If you decide to focus on previous clients, evaluate which clients have been most profitable in the past, and where you've had a good experience. Do you want to work with them again? Determine which clients have the potential for new growth and new projects. You might include in your plan to conduct client satisfaction interviews with previous clients. In addition to asking, "How did we do? What could we have done better?" you can ask where their challenges will be over the next year and how you might be of support in the future. Then listen carefully to everything they have to say. We will discuss client satisfaction interviews in more detail in chapter 9 when we talk about building client loyalty thru communication.

- **Define Your Company's Perfect Client.** Now determine what your perfect client would look like in each of the sectors you have chosen. Define the criteria for the types of clients you want to work with on upcoming projects. Some of the criteria for defining the perfect client for your company might be:
  - o They have a need for your services.
  - o Their projects can be profitable.
  - o They are a good fit for your skills and services.
  - o They understand the value you bring.
  - o You understand their business.
  - o You have the opportunity for an internal champion.
  - o A trusting relationship has been or can be established.
  - o A similar corporate structure and values exists between the two companies.
  - o The company is financially stable and will fairly and timely compensate its business partners (they pay their bills).

Identify Target Prospects. Once your sectors have been determined and you have defined the perfect client, then you will develop a list of potential clients in each sector. The number of targets you choose will be determined by the size of your Business Development team and the time they have available. When you have your list of good prospective clients, then move on to develop a plan for each of those targets.

Gather as much basic information as you can about each individual prospective target. This exercise helps you gain an understanding of how best to pursue *them*. There are all kinds of prospect tracking tools, but keep it simple in the beginning.

Included at the end of chapter 8 is a good form that can be used for tracking prospective client information. The form also becomes your Capture Plan for moving the prospect through the steps from being *target* to becoming a *new client* with whom you have established a strong relationship. If you will follow the steps in the process, you will end up with a strong client relationship. A strong relationship greatly increases your chances of gaining new work with this prospect. Store the information in a central location so that all of the Business Development team members have access to the same information.

A word about confidentiality: You may want to restrict access only to certain people for your Business Development plan and target information. This valuable information might inadvertently get into the wrong hands and thus negate your competitive advantage. Your competitors would love to know what you are planning to do!

For each prospective client, obtain all the pertinent information, such as names of key people, locations, type of business, what their problems and issues might be, and any upcoming opportunities. Then identify possible ways to meet the decision makers in the company. You might try to obtain referrals from a similar type of client, or someone who is familiar with business. You might check internally—it can be surprising who has connections to your targets. LinkedIn and other media sites can provide additional personal information.

Finding the real decision-maker in an organization is one of the most difficult and most important tasks about contacting new prospects. Be mindful of the person's position in the organization, and whether or not that person is a decision-maker or can be of help in connecting you to the right person. Make sure he or she is the right person before spending time trying to establish a relationship.

Conduct enough research on the company and their industry to understand their business. Pay attention to any hints of upcoming projects. Analyze how your company might be a fit and how you can offer the services they might need. Try to determine where the growth is in the organization. Check their website, their annual report, and the CEO's address. Even the budget may contain useful information about future projects. A word of warning: Don't allow yourself to get lost in the research process. It may feel like you are doing Business Development, but such activity can be a serious time-waster. Obtain just enough information to know if it is worthwhile to pursue this target. Stay focused on accomplishing your goal of finding a way to meet and talk with the decision-maker at the target company—that is when true Business Development begins.

RFPs and RFQs. Include in this section of your plan, the criteria for any solicitations you will pursue. If there is not a predefined criterion, then you will tend to waste resources going after everything—especially if you are not currently busy. At other times, you may pass up great opportunities because you are too busy to put together a response. This is not a good way to do business. Responding to solicitations that are not a good fit can be costly in both time and billability. Stick with your plan and focus on your targets. Go/No-Go decisions will become much clearer when you do.

Highly successful companies differentiate themselves by adamantly sticking to a predefined criterion for choosing clients and responses. It is how they choose to work *smarter.*

Before responding to a solicitation, determine if:

- This company is in your target sector.
- This prospect is a good target client.
- There an existing relationship or if you have at least met with someone in the company.

- The project would be a good fit for your company services.
- You were aware of the RFP before it was public knowledge—prior knowledge proves a trusted relationship with the prospective client.
- There is reasonable time for the response.
  - o When the response timeframe is short, it could mean that the solicitation was written with another firm in mind and the decision has already been made.
  - o They may be soliciting for proposals because they are required to do so by law.
  - o They may just want to make sure they are getting the best price. Some companies have been known to use your proposal rates to negotiate with their preferred provider!
  - o If the time allowed for putting together a response is reasonable, then they might truly be looking for new ideas and alternatives.

Define The Schedule and the Process. The Business Development process begins once a target prospect has been named. You will then determine how and where to meet the decision-makers. A good place to meet them might be at a networking event—schedule those meetings and events on your calendar. Less effective, but sometimes necessary, is to make a cold call to introduce yourself and your company, and then follow up with information about your company. Contact them again to set up a meeting. When you do get a meeting, outline the questions that you will use to guide the conversation. Then follow up again and again. Again, it may take six to nine times before you begin to see results. If you are unable to make contact this week, put it on your calendar for next week. We will go into more detail about this process in future chapters.

Staying in touch with previous clients should also be built into the schedule. A client retention program is part of the necessary Business Development follow-up. Define that process in your plan, especially after a job or project is completed. Make sure a client satisfaction interview is conducted and that future concerns or upcoming projects for the client are recorded and addressed.

Section 4—Networking and Tradeshow Activities. Outline time for networking efforts in your plan. Meetings should be placed on the calendar as appointments. Networking is very important to the overall Business Development effort and should be mapped out in advance.

Networking works because it puts you on a professional level with prospective clients and your peers. It's just a great way to meet people that you would have difficulty getting in to see any other way. A quick rule of thumb for determining which networking opportunities would be best for your firm is if your competitor is there, you probably should be there, too. If your targeted client is there, you definitely should be there.

List all the networking events that are a possibility. Narrow it down to those that make sense for your business and consider the amount of time available. Your team will not be able to attend them all. Once the events have been decided, prioritize them. A good way to prioritize is to put them into A, B, and C categories.

The A group is those that must be attended and you keep them on your schedule. The B group is important, but other things might periodically keep you from attending, such as a client meeting. For the C group, attend if you have available time. Everybody in the company should participate in at least one networking organization.

It is worthwhile to also participate in networking organizations that are mostly attended by your peers. Interacting with peers can provide teaming opportunities and you can learn from each other. If you carry a heavy workload, try to focus the majority of your time on those organizations where target clients will be attending.

You will be much more effective if you don't try to take on too many networking groups. It works best to become involved and known in the group; it gives you more credibility. Volunteer for an office, work on committees, give papers—do anything to be visible and to participate. Promote your company's professional image. In your plan, determine who in your office will be responsible for attending each of the various networking opportunities that have been chosen. If the assigned person is unable to attend, then it is their responsibility to find an alternate team member to attend in their absence, particularly for the A-category events.

Section 5—Implementation

The implementation of the Business Development plan applies to the individual—this is where the rubber meets the road. All the great planning you've done is worthless without successful implementation.

Break the plan into parts, and name who will be responsible for implementing and monitoring each part. This decision depends on which team member has that particular area of knowledge and will determine where they target their Business Development time. Working smart means it doesn't take a lot of time to do Business Development—just clear objectives, dedication, persistence and consistent follow-up. Who you assign will also depend on who is dependable enough to be trusted with this very important segment of your target marketing. Once parts have been assigned, team members need to understand that the responsibility will not be picked up by anyone else—so give it some thought before making assignments.

The Team. In this section, name who will be on your marketing team and what their areas of responsibility will be. If you have enough people, it works well to have each individual be responsible for a different sector or type of business.

Map out how much time is to be spent on Business Development each day. This is especially important if your personnel are highly billable. How much time does each team member have available for Business Development? It is best to have everyone stick to a schedule, even if it is only for a few minutes each day. It needs to be spelled out so that everyone understands their responsibilities. Too often, Business Development happens only when there is nothing else to do—which of course is never going to work very well.

Choose one person to lead the Business Development effort, to act as the driver. This person will make sure that the plan is followed and that nothing falls through the cracks. That doesn't mean this person does all the work; it just means that he or she makes sure everyone is doing what they said they would do by coordinating, tracking leads, and monitoring the Business Development activities. This can be the person that leads the weekly Business Development discussions.

Determine who will be responsible for monitoring and researching websites. This person will search for RFP postings for the targeted prospects and clients that you have listed in the plan.

Everyone in the office should know what Business Development projects each team member is working on so that potential clients do not receive mixed messages by having more than one individual contact them. Meet regularly as a group to discuss progress, encourage and motivate each other, and to hold each other accountable for doing what you set out to do.

The Personal Plan. The company's Business Development plan must then be implemented on a personal level. Here is an example of a personal plan:

Joe, a senior engineer, has knowledge of a particular area or service that the company provides. He wishes to expand that service area, and so he takes on the responsibility to develop new business around that service. In the Business Development plan, Joe is named as the team member responsible for the sector.

He might start with a simple table or spreadsheet matrix that helps him organize information, crystallize his focus, and track his accomplishments. It helps him create a consistent focus and prevents lapses that could cause the "feast or famine" effect—all while maintaining billability.

Joe can list all the companies that he is responsible for targeting, determine how far out he can realistically reach geographically, conduct the research on potential clients, and build a schedule of when he will contact them and what he will discuss. He will track his activities and report back to the group each week. He attends networking events that fit that sector and where prospective clients might be attending. The key is to find a way to be where they are and to meet them.

Joe will develop a monthly calendar of whom he is going to contact, and when. He should give himself deadlines for contacting his prospective targets. It is important to be persistent and to set milestones.

With new prospective clients, the goal is to set up a face-to-face introductory meeting which will begin establishing a relationship. With existing clients, he is focused on finding ways to expand services to them. Joe's goal with previous clients is to reestablish contact and to find out if they have new projects coming up.

The purpose of having a detailed personal Business Development plan is to create a clear focus and to help Joe avoid a common pitfall of Business Development—busywork. He will learn that it is better to make a few good calls to defined targets than it is to make a bunch of useless calls. It is important to keep the target list short and focused, and to continue working the list until he gets in to see those people. Since Joe is highly billable, talking to five quality prospects a week is a good goal. That is just one each day; anyone should be able to do that, no matter how busy.

Reporting back weekly is important because it is motivational and creates a sense of urgency. It gives Joe a scorecard and a place to brag about his efforts, and to receive constructive input and guidance that might be helpful.

This is Joe's personal Business Development plan. Joe learns quickly that while planning is important, he cannot get stuck in the process. He must keep it simple, limit how much time he spends on research and planning, and move on to the *real action* part of the plan: making contact and establishing a relationship with the targeted potential client.

Section 6—Budget Planning. The final piece of your plan is determining a budget.

The average small professional services firm should expect to spend 5 to 10 percent of revenue on marketing and Business Development. That may seem like a lot, until you realize that retail typically spends more than 25 percent of their revenue on searching for new business. Spending more on Business Development activities can dramatically increase the results as long as the money is spent in the right place.

It's smart to spend your financial resources on finding the type of clients you need and really want to work with in order to grow your business.

Promote the services that are profitable and those that differentiate you from the competition. If you are trying to grow in a highly competitive market, then you will need to spend more money. You should expect to spend more if you are going after a sector that requires more entertainment or other types of expenditures, so keep all that in mind as you prepare your budget. If you are a start-up, then a large portion of your budget in the first years will go toward branding, or the process of building your image in such places as website design and promotional materials.

Some companies worry too much about the costs of doing something when they should be concerned about the cost of doing nothing—or not doing enough—to grow their business.

How much new business should you strive for each year? A simple calculation can give you the answer.

1. Targeted annual revenue amount $_____
2. Forecast from current clients $_____
3. Additional revenue required (line 1 minus 2) $_____
4. Estimate expected revenue loss
   (due to attrition, competition, lack of funding, etc.) $_____
5. Total new revenue required (line 3 plus 4) $_____

New revenue required from line 5 is your minimum target number for the year. From this simple calculation you have the number that you will back in to when determining the activity level required to find new work.

Some believe that a 20 percent increase in business each year is necessary just to stay even. In order to stay ahead of inflation and to allow for the unexpected loss of a key client or market shifts, you may need to make adjustments throughout the year.

To begin your budget planning, evaluate everything you did last year that produced positive results. If you are a start-up, then you may have some hits and misses while you evaluate various options. If your business is a few years old, make sure you know where marketing and Business Development dollars are being spent. Marketing budgets must be planned and controlled, or they can get out of hand very quickly.

Do you know the activities that produced positive results? Knowing your proposal win rate, and the amount of activity it took to capture existing work, will help determine the level of activity necessary to reach your revenue target. The most cost-effective use of your Business Development spending is with existing clients. Interact with them often. Work hard to make sure they are happy, and constantly try to find ways to expand your service offerings with them.

Stay focused on your target market when deciding where to spend your financial resources. It's easy to become distracted by an opportunity that calls the loudest but may not be a primary target. It is not necessary to ignore those opportunities, but just know that these are your secondary targets and spend your resources accordingly. Narrowing your focus will allow you to have a much greater impact with fewer dollars. That's why the planning process is so important. Having a clear plan for where the marketing budget goes translates into more high-quality leads for the money spent.

Accounting. Marketing and Business Development expense accounting can be as elaborate as you wish, but it might be best to keep it simple in the beginning. Build in some flexibility. Some years you will spend more in a particular area and more in other areas the next year. There are a number of budget planning methods that can be used to track Business Development and marketing expenses. For some firms it might work best to use a combination, depending on the amount of revenue.

- **The Projection Method** works well if the company is stable and has historical numbers to use as a reference, and if the marketing efforts remain the same for most years. This method is thought of as something of a mathematical exercise because it fails to consider the variances in conditions of the market and changes in marketing focus throughout the year.

- **The Percentage Method** is used to allocate a certain percentage of the firm's revenue to marketing. This method can work well if the firm is stable and does not plan to make large changes or to pursue new markets.

- **The Goal-Based Method** is the most realistic and accurate method of budget planning. This method allows you to base your planning on the actual goals of the firm's business plan for the year. Using your Business Development and Marketing plan, you will determine the funding requirements to complete each of the identified tasks. Once you have priced out all that you wish to accomplish, you may determine that available funding is just not there, or you might find funding that allows you to do more than you thought. Either way, at least you know for sure what the budget needs to look like, and you can plan accordingly. You can take the final number and compare it to prior years for a historical comparison, and you might also compare it to industry standards to see how your firm compares.

- **Tracking expenses**. The more defined you can be about the costs you will incur, the more accurate your budgeting will be. You must consider the effect on the bottom line for the current year as well as for the future of the company. Monitoring your expenditures can be as precise as you choose to make it. Some firms wish to monitor monthly; others feel that quarterly is sufficient.

In order to monitor and track your marketing and Business Development costs accurately, expenses should be matched to an itemized list and have their own cost codes. Specific marketing expenditures can be assigned numbers, just as with any other item costing. Each type of activity can have a predetermined cost code which allows you to see where the most activity is being focused. You can regularly pull reports and make adjustments where needed. By assigning financial codes, you take advantage of the financial system already in place for your firm. Professional staff members will record marketing time on their time sheets using set cost codes, just as they do for billable project time.

Direct and Indirect Costs. Direct costs will be the largest expenditures of your marketing budget, from 50 to70 percent. Direct costs will be items such as personnel costs for Business Development and marketing professionals, as well as time technical professionals dedicate to Business Development. Calculate the hourly rate for the time technical professionals charge to marketing for proposal development, meetings, presentations, and planning.

Indirect costs will be almost everything else related to marketing, and can sometimes be difficult to contain. These costs would be for such items as networking registrations, tradeshows, website, social media, outsourced expertise (such as for website maintenance), subscriptions, entertainment of clients and prospects, printing, promotional items, business gifts, postage, sponsorships, public relations, donations, supplies, and maybe a few technology gadgets.

Website. One of the best investments you can make with your marketing budget is to build or update your firm's website. This is your image—the way the world sees you. The image should be consistent and the message clear. Include website upgrades and maintenance in this section of the budget. If you have not updated your website in a while, you may need to plan for about 50 percent of your marketing budget to go toward building a powerful lead-generating website, depending on the type of business you are in.

Networking should be at the top of the priority list. The more expensive networking opportunities may not be the best. A little research will prove that there are many organizations that are not costly and the same potential contacts are attending. Remember to include lodging and travel costs when estimating this number.

Brochures and Print Advertising. The traditional marketing approach of using brochures can be a very big expense, and it is difficult to show the actual return on your investment. If you have a strong web presence it may not be necessary. Print advertising can also be very expensive, and most professional services firms feel that the short-term return is not there. It just depends on your service offering. If you decide to use print advertising, chose publications that reach your target audience and keep in mind that the repeated message is most effective. When done consistently printed advertising is useful for building brand awareness over time, but may not be an effective way to generate leads or short-term returns for the professional services firm.

Education and Training Expenses. Providing Business Development training for all staff that will be interacting with clients and prospects is crucial, but can be expensive. Technical staff members are in the best position to identify new opportunities with existing clients. Technical professionals are sometimes so focused on the project that Business Development is secondary on their minds. They may miss opportunities without training to help them recognize an opportunity when it is presented and to know what to do about it. Business Development training of technical professionals can make a very big difference in the growth of any firm, so be sure there is a place in your budget to include training costs.

Marketing and Business Development is expensive. How this chunk of your revenue is spent should be well thought-out and planned. If not, it can spin out of control quickly. Ultimately the measurement of success will be the measurement of results versus cost. If it can't be measured, then it can't be managed. Keep accurate records of how the marketing budget is being spent—that's the only true method of determining how your business is doing.

Finally—Stay Flexible. As you implement your Business Development Plan, you may find that some things work and others do not, so be flexible. Spend your time on those things that are working, and change what you can that is not working. Continuously make sure you are on target and review the plan at least quarterly. Make necessary directional changes and updates annually, keeping in mind that your plan is intended to be a living document. Adjust it accordingly.

Implementation of the Business Development Plan

One of the problems many companies run into at this point is that they feel so good about completing the planning process that they pat themselves on the back for a job well done. They tend to forget that the implementation phase is the most important part of the process. Implementation of the plan is the key to bringing in new project opportunities for the firm.

Here are a few pointers that might help:

- **Don't try to do everything at once**—The more there is to do, the less likely *anything* will get done. Break implementation of your plan into small manageable chunks that can be managed along with other day-to-day tasks. Set priorities in order to avoid the tensions of competing areas of responsibilities.

- **Make assignments**—Staff can share Business Development responsibilities, but make sure everyone is clear on what their responsibilities are and the expected outcomes.
- **Meet regularly**—Schedule weekly meetings with your leaders to discuss progress. If you are a sole owner, set aside time each week to review progress. Progress meetings will ensure that team members are maintaining a focus on the goals and are committed to achieving them. Without these regularly scheduled meetings, employees will succumb to their natural tendencies—namely, to focus on the day-to-day tasks of running of the business.
- **Measure and monitor progress**—Tracking progress consistently will give staff feedback and support, and will also ensure accountability.
- **Recognize and reward positive progress often**—Transparent reporting of results will provide your project teams with the visibility to see measureable progress and to appreciate how they have contributed to the achievement of the organization's objectives.

Building a workable Business Development plan is a step-by-step process. Take your time, brainstorm with others, and evaluate the reality of implementing each step. Remember this is not a masterpiece, but a reference document. It is a guide to be used every day. Work through each section of the planning process completely.

If done correctly, this plan is a tool that you will be working with for a long time. Business Development is a habit to be cultivated by investing time and energy into managing the process. The first step in managing that process is constructing the Business Development plan, but the next step of implementation is crucial. When executed properly, your Business Development plan will produce dramatic results. Results of your activity will be stronger than ever before—and your business will thrive long term. You will be working smarter instead of working harder.

Key Concepts in this Chapter

1. No matter how small, every company must have a Business Development Plan. That's where it all begins.

2. Conduct a SWOT analysis. Determine strengths and weakness of the firm and evaluate any opportunities or threats in the market place.

3. Know what the perfect client looks like for your firm's capabilities.

4. Determine the best industry sectors and client types for the services your firm provides.

5. Develop a budget for Business Development and marketing.

6. Outline how the plan will be implemented and who will be involved.

7. Encourage individuals to develop their own personal plan for how they will spend their Business Development time.

5

THE BRAINSTORMING SESSION GUIDE

The development of your Business Development plan begins with a brainstorming session. Brainstorming can be a very effective way to get started, because it is not one person's creativity that is working but several. Ideally, those people will all have different backgrounds and areas of expertise. Coming up with creative ideas and thoughts can be fun and exciting, especially when you gather a variety of thinkers to focus on a plan for the future of the business.

Participants. Depending on the size of your firm, ask at least the key people in your organization to participate. People with different responsibilities and from different departments can add a variety of ideas to the mix. New employees can contribute the perspectives of their previous employers.

Everybody who is involved in selling the firm's professional services should have a voice and be involved in the planning process. Gather your key folks away from office distractions and ban the cell phones. If you are a single business owner, find some dedicated time to think and record your thoughts.

Brainstorming is designed to jar the brain into thinking of new ideas and approaches to gaining new business. As ideas spill from the brain and are vocalized, a facilitator captures the nuggets on a board or flip chart. A brainstorming session for Business Development ideas has the potential to determine best practices, create new marketing concepts, and stimulate enthusiasm for the Business Development process.

Build and expand on the ideas of others and add extra thoughts to each idea. Use other people's ideas as inspiration for your own. Creative people are also good listeners. Combine several of the suggested ideas to explore new possibilities. It's just as valuable to be able to adapt and improve on other people's ideas as it is to generate the initial idea that sets off new trains of thought.

Every person has a valid viewpoint and a unique perspective on the situation in a constructive brainstorming session. You can always throw out ideas purely to spark off other people's ideas and not just as a final thought. Encourage participation from everyone. It is the group's responsibility to ensure that all participants feel able to contribute freely and confidently. It's usually best to have at least three people, but not more than twenty people. If the group is too large, some may feel less confident about offering their thoughts and ideas. Do not allow anyone to dominate the conversation. Ask for feedback from individuals who might be shy. A creative environment is one where people feel comfortable in expressing their ideas and where constructive support is given in the development and analysis of those ideas.

Choose a Facilitator. Whomever you choose to be the moderator, be it yourself or someone else, he or she should be an outgoing, social person who is familiar with providing direction in a non-authoritarian manner. The facilitator's job is to guide the process and encourage everyone to participate, to dismiss nothing, and to prevent others from pouring scorn on the wilder suggestions. The facilitator can diplomatically combine or include the weaker ideas within other themes to avoid dismissing or rejecting contributions.

The capture and documentation of all ideas is paramount to a successful operation. Don't rely on memory; write down ideas as quickly as they are given. Consider using easel pads with adhesive on the back; that way each section of discussion can be captured and then attached to the wall (without harm) so that participants can view and refer to them as necessary.

It's the facilitator's job to help people turn their unformed ideas into reality by giving encouragement and suggestions and by asking helpful questions. Great ideas are born during brainstorming sessions, but without follow-up they will be lost. Don't allow a lull to stop the process. Give attendees a moment to gather thoughts before abandoning an idea. The silence will eventually be broken and the best ideas might be yet to come. If yours is a small company, most likely the facilitator will be the owner or a business development manager. Be careful not to automatically place one of these people in this role. Someone else might be a better fit, and the owner or business development manager might contribute more as a participant than as a facilitator. Brainstorming places a significant burden on the facilitator to manage the process, people's involvement and sensitivities, and the follow-up actions.

As you prepare for a brainstorming meeting, keep integration and the decision-making process in mind. Follow guidelines for meeting structure and brainstorming techniques with an open mind. Ideas will come or not.

Choose a Creative Environment. The environment for the meeting is important. Choose a location away from distractions. Designate cell phone time and ask that they be turned off at other times. Creativity works best in quiet and uninterrupted atmospheres.

Keep the brainstorming session simple and allocate a time limit for each section. This will enable you to keep the random brainstorming activity under control and on track. Ensure that everyone participating in the brainstorming session understands and agrees on the time frame, aim, and purpose of the session.

A brainstorming meeting may last as long as a couple of hours, or it could last for a couple of days. Comfortable chairs, water, juice, coffee, tea, and snacks set a welcoming and relaxed atmosphere. The facilitator and participants can use whiteboards and large pads on easels with multicolored markers to spark creativity. So they are aware of expectations, participants should know the meeting is to generate creative solutions and is part of the larger decision-making process.

Encourage Creativity. Brainstorming is nonlinear with creativity and inspiration following their own timetables; you cannot force them. Teams gather to generate creative ideas in what amounts to a social project. Let minds run free and see where it all goes. Enable people to suggest ideas at random. People should feel comfortable throwing out ideas and not be afraid to change the topic or say something unconventional. Another factor in brainstorming meetings is relaxation. Try some icebreakers to get everyone warmed up. Icebreakers set a relaxed tone at the beginning of the meeting and help participants step out of their cubicles and think outside the box.

Brainstorming with a group of people is a powerful technique—creating new ideas, solving problems, motivating staff and developing teamwork by making them feel a part of the bigger picture. Brainstorming motivates because it involves members of a team in bigger management issues, and it gets a team working together to grow the company.

Discuss what kind of firm you want to be and determine how much growth you can realistically handle each year. Firms with a clear strategy—built on their strengths and differentiators—tend to grow faster in a more manageable way and are more profitable.

Guide for Conducting a Brainstorming Session

Use this format as a guide for your brainstorming session. Work through one section at a time and record discussion points before moving to the next section. Easel pads with adhesive across the back work well to record each section as they can be stuck to the wall around the room for reference as you work through the process.

The following is a suggested outline for your Business Development plan brainstorming session. This should take three to five hours, depending on how much detail and discussion takes place.

1. Purpose   (10 minutes)

Spend about ten minutes explaining the purpose of this brainstorming exercise which is to develop a defined Business Development and marketing plan. The plan will be the road map for growth and will contain *goals* and *objectives.*

Without a clear vision and plan, people tend to go in many different directions and will actually work harder but accomplish less.

Define the timeframe and items to be covered:

- o where we want to go and how we will get there
- o our strengths and weakness
- o where we see future opportunities
- o what additional services can we offer to existing clients
- o what the prefect client for our company looks like
- o sectors where we plan to focus
- o specific target clients within those sectors
- o things we can do as individuals that can contribute to marketing efforts for the company

Explain that brainstorming is designed to jar the brain into thinking new thoughts and creating new ideas. Everybody participates and is critical to the process so all input, suggestions, and ideas are welcome. One person's idea may stimulate an idea from someone else. There is no wrong answer. The only wrong is to not participate.

2. Define Direction of the Company with a Mission and Vision Statement (30 minutes)

"Mission Statements" and "Vision Statements" do two distinctly different jobs.

What is our *mission*?

- Created first
- Defines our success
- Describes our purpose

You may be able to pull this from the company's business plan. A mission statement defines the organization's purpose and primary objectives. Its prime function is *internal*—to define the key measure or measures of the organization's success—and its prime audience is the leadership team and stockholders of the company.

Example: "Our mission is to be the preferred provider of quality engineering solutions to our clients."

What is our *vision* for the future of the company?

- Where are we headed?
- What do we want to become?
- Who are we?
- What do we stand for?

Vision statements also define the organization's purpose, but this time in terms of the organization's values rather than bottom-line measures.

Values are guiding beliefs about how things should be done. It encompasses both the purpose and values of the organization. For employees, it gives direction about how they are expected to behave, and inspires them to give their best. *Shared with customers*, it shapes customers' understanding of why they should work with the organization. It's the human value.

Example: "To be recognized by our clients as a trusted partner. To provide our employees with challenging projects and a secure, stable environment in which to build their careers."

3. Conduct a SWOT analysis to help identify   (1 hour)

- Strengths
- Weaknesses/Limitations
- Opportunities
- Threats

A SWOT analysis will give your planning efforts more clarity and is necessary for future planning.

Strengths: characteristics of the business, or project team that give it an advantage over others

> Examples: veteran-owned, president involved in projects, known for expertise in ___., diversity of disciplines, small and flexible, responsive, already known in certain areas, low overhead

Weaknesses (or Limitations): characteristics that place the team at a disadvantage relative to others

> Examples: small company, perception of the client is that we lack experienced professionals or may not be able to deal with large projects

Opportunities: external chances to improve performance and make greater profits in the current environment

> Examples: new company starting from the beginning means no negatives to overcome, economy improving so clients will have budgets for new projects

Threats: external elements in the environment that could cause trouble for the business or project

> Examples: lots of competition in the federal market, lack of funding in the municipalities

4. Identify Business Sectors and Prospective Targets (1 hour)

Target Market Sectors

Let the group help determine what type of client makes the best and most profitable sectors to target for the skill set of the technical professionals. Brainstorming can reveal new target markets where additional project work can be obtained. Create a list of untapped demographics and have people brainstorm ideas and approaches that could be effective. Additionally, brainstorm new services that could be potential fits for these new markets. Encourage those involved in Business Development to make calls to the newly identified markets and collect feedback to be discussed at a future brainstorming session.

What sectors will we target and what services will we provide to each sector?

Name the industry sectors that are most likely to buy your services. This is where your Business Development efforts will be focused. This section will take the most time to work through. Ask these questions:

- What is our expertise?
- What is the extent of our experience?
- Could we add a sector by making a key new hire?
- Assign a manager for each sector who will learn everything about that sector.

Name Target Prospective Clients

- Identify potential new clients in each sector that you serve.
- Assign a manager for each target client.
    o What does the perfect client look like for us?
    o Develop a plan for each targeted client.

Existing Clients that Need To Be Nurtured Further

Evaluate the top 20 percent of revenue producers. How can you expand services to them? Discuss ideas.

- Conduct satisfaction interviews.
- Offer client training workshops.
- Ask them about future plans.

5. Where Will We Market and Who Will Be Responsible?　　　(30 minutes)

Geographic Reach

- What geographic area can we realistically serve?
- Possible acquisitions of similar or complementary firms that would provide access to new geographic regions.

How the Plan Will Be Implemented

The Marketing Team

a. Identify number of hours each person has for marketing efforts outside of proposal-writing time.

b. Determine how often the group will meet to track and discuss progress. Business Development meetings can be scheduled to discuss progress on assigned targets. How often you meet will depend on the size of your firm, and how often you meet on other occasions when such discussions might occur. Discussions focused on Business Development help to motivate and guide efforts.

c. Obtain commitment to the plan and make sure expectations are clear.

d. You can get as detailed as you want here, even to the point of defining the number of calls and prospective client meetings each person is required to hold each week.

6. Conferences and Tradeshows   (30 minutes)

List conference and tradeshows that you plan to attend. This decision should be determined by where potential and existing clients will attend. Include the associated costs such as exhibit fees, and travel and lodging costs. It may not be necessary to exhibit at all conferences attended; there is often value in just attending and networking with people.

Networking Activities   (30 minutes)

The purpose of networking is to meet potential new clients or teaming partners. It is the easiest way to meet a number of people at once. Attendees are there to meet others, and are more receptive at these events to talking with those that they do not yet know. Refer to chapter 6 for more information on networking.

First, develop a list of all possible organizations. (Do this before the brainstorming session in order to give staff time to consider interests.) Choose the ones of interest and rank them (**A, B, or C**) in order of priority. Then name who will be responsible for each networking organization.

A—*Most important*—Your potential clients or teaming partners will attend these organization events. The meeting is on your calendar as an appointment because you must go. You must attend and participate; if for some reason you cannot attend, then you will get someone else to attend in your place. You have responsibilities in the organization, on a committee or participating in another way.

B—*Important but not crucial*—Events may be more related to networking with peers or for earning continuing education credits. Attend if at all possible.

C—*Good to attend when possible* but not a priority for helping with Business Development objectives.

7. Additional information that supports the Business Development Plan   (1hour)

Information Management

Decide how marketing and Business Development information will be managed. All marketing information and leads must be managed in order to be useful at a future date. Technology can make life much easier and your marketing planning will take on a new clarity once you have a system in place that works for you.

Additional Marketing Options

Discuss other ideas for ongoing marketing efforts that might create brand recognition and awareness for the company. It is important to maintain brand consistency in all efforts. Technical professional staff can contribute for many of these:

- website
- press releases
- direct mail (e-mails)
- newsletters
- white papers
- advertising
- sponsorships
- vendor registrations
- website upgrades
- LinkedIn searches
- blogs on the website
- testimonials
- client satisfaction interviews
- standardized branding

Other Possibilities—such as federal, state and local registrations

8. Education and Staff Training Needs

In this section, discuss ongoing or one-time education needs of internal staff. Education should be offered continuously as a refresher and to provide new motivation for Business Development activities. Essential training for technical professionals would include:

- networking skills
- proposal development and short-list presentations
- communication skills

9. The Budget Plan   (30 minutes)

This section comes last, because you need to know what you plan to do before you can determine costs.

- Spend time estimating costs of the activities you plan.
- Look at what certain activities cost last year.
- What can you add? What should you give up because the results did not prove it to be effective?

If you find that there are things you would like to do but the cost is prohibitive for this year, move it to a long-term plan. Keep the current plan realistic, clean, and focused.

10. Finally, Write The Plan

Discuss any other elements of the plan that you wish to include and make sure everyone understands their roles in the final preparation of the Business Development plan and how the information will be used.

When the brainstorming session is complete, gather all easel-pad pages from the wall, keeping them in order, and sit down to write your plan. You can designate someone else to do the writing, as long as they attended the meeting and understand the intentions for the information.

Write the plan while everything is fresh on your mind. You will find it comes fairly easily, since you have all the information you need in front of you. When your draft is complete, you may want to run it by others that attended to make sure you captured everything. Schedule a meeting to review and discuss implementation, roles and responsibilities, and timeframes for each activity.

<u>Key Concepts in this Chapter</u>

1. A brainstorming session is the best way to start the development of your Business Development Plan.
2. This chapter provides a timed guide for facilitating the brainstorming session.

3. Involve key people in the firm that can offer many different perspectives.
4. Conduct the brainstorming sessions away from distractions and allow plenty of time for ideas to develop.
5. Encourage creativity by allowing everyone to feel safe about expressing their opinions and ideas.

6

NETWORKING

Networking is an important Business Development activity that is especially valuable to those in the professional services industry. In addition to meeting prospective clients, networking activities can create opportunities for the exchange of information, ideas, and technical resources. If you could identify one area to concentrate on that would significantly impact the growth of your business, it would be networking. Compared to the amount of time and money it requires, it is one of the most productive and most powerful forms of marketing available to you.

It's not enough for your firm to just do "excellent work." That's a given—it is expected. You must get out in the world and expose people to the excellent services that you can provide. People do business with people. So pack up your business cards and get out of the office!

Networking is a noun that means arrangement of intersections or interactions. It can open the doors for new business opportunities with prospective clients that you do not know but might meet at organized functions. Such opportunities work best when you're striving to make connections that will lead to building long-term professional relationships. There are all kinds of opportunities to network with your target market, or to meet people who can introduce you to them. Networking can be part of your community and social activities, or you can focus on attending meetings and conferences of various professional trade organizations. Your plan could include a combination of several.

The Rule of 250. Here's an interesting fact about networking. If you know 250 people, you can generally find out about anything just by making a few phone calls. These people are your bank of resources. Everybody has a different network of people they know, and by knowing these 250 people, you also have access to their networks!

Keep in mind that networking events are not for selling. Effective networking is more about meeting new people and developing relationships. Selling professional services is usually relationship-driven, and networking events provide a great place to begin to establish a connection that can lead to a relationship with a future client. Networking is defined as more of a farming activity than a hunting activity.

Benefits of Networking. A networking event increases your *visibility* to prospective clients, and furthers your *credibility* with the people you already know. Networking is also a good way to keep up with industry trends. Best of all, networking does away with the need to make cold calls, because you will attend meetings where you can meet your prospective new clients. Cold calling is one of the worst ways to build your business; time would be better spent attending networking events. You will be meeting people on their own levels. The goal for networking is to meet as many people as possible in order to gain a direct or indirect connection with the person you want to get to know. It creates an atmosphere that is much warmer and more personable than cold calling or e-mailing.

When you meet people at a networking event that you want to get to know better, set up a time to meet with them face-to-face. When you ask for a meeting, your purpose is to learn more about what they do and how you might be able to help them. The most effective way to build a relationship with a prospective client is to find ways to be helpful to them first before asking for anything. It may seem counterintuitive—but it works.

People Do Business with People. Meeting more people will mean creating more leads for the type of work that is right for your business. The more people you know, the more likely you are to find the connection you need in order to chase a particular opportunity, or to find someone to introduce you to a prospective target client. People prefer to do business with people they know and trust. The more people you can get to share in your business community, the more opportunities you have to develop relationships of trust and respect. Those relationships will help to grow your business through word-of-mouth referrals.

Different Types of Networking

You have many choices when it comes to networking opportunities. However, you have only so many hours available in each day so you must choose wisely. The different types of networking are:

1. professional organizations
2. peers and those people you already know
3. social situations and events
4. conferences and tradeshows

Each type of networking opportunity provides a different set of benefits.

Professional Trade Organizations. Become involved in a professional organization that interests you. When you are willing to invest time and energy in helping an organization, you enrich the experience for others and help the community of your industry to grow. You are considered a contributor and will gain credibility in your industry. People want to be around those who contribute and make a difference. It becomes a positive experience for everyone and improves the organization.

Professional organizations are an excellent way to meet your targeted client, but choose your networking options carefully in order to be able to spend the time required. Networking is a selfless activity with great payoffs if you choose the right organizations. How do you decide where to spend your time?

First, compile a list of every possible networking organization for your industry, focusing on those that hold meetings in your area. A good place to start your list is to ask clients and potential clients about the events they find helpful. What organizations do your competitors find beneficial? Where do they spend their time? Ask your friends and peers where they discover the best opportunities to meet prospective clients.

Next, rank or categorize the networking events according to priority: A, B, or C.

- **A**—This is an organization that is recognized as *important* to your profession. It is a client-rich environment—your existing or potential clients are there. The meeting is placed on your calendar as an appointment and you are committed to attending. You will actively participate by holding an office or becoming part of a committee. This one is so important that if you are not able to attend, you recruit someone to attend in your place.
- **B**—You have it scheduled and will make the meetings unless something much more important such as a client meeting preempts it.
- **C**—You will attend if you can. These events may be more peer networking or social in nature. It would be good to be there, but not imperative.

You can further rank them within each category. Your rankings may change as you learn more about various organizations. Some groups are a good prospective client mining resource in one area, but may not be as good in other areas. Other groups will be good for interacting with potential teaming partners or peers.

Attending every networking opportunity can be very time consuming if not managed carefully. The positive trade-off is that it can open many doors that would be difficult to open any other way. People attending the event are there to network and are more willing to take the time to visit. Most everyone is impressed with a person who *wants* to meet them. Networking events should be considered a means to meet a number of people at once and not to "do business."

Work the Event. To some people, networking can be difficult. They cringe when thinking about going to a networking event and meeting new people. Some will even look for a corner to hide in as soon as they arrive. That's too bad, because it is such a fantastic opportunity to further your business.

Working a networking event is an art form in itself. Here are some pointers that might help to make the most of the opportunity:

- Keep in mind that this is valuable time, so have a plan, such as a set number of people that you want to speak with. With each person, say hello and spend about five minutes introducing yourself and a little about your company. Exchange business cards, and if you have determined this is someone worth knowing better, suggest that you get together another time for more conversation. Set a time to call, and then move on to another person.
- Take the time before you go to a networking event to compose a condensed description of the kind of work your firm does and

your role. Some call this the ten-second elevator speech. Writing it out and reading it over in advance will help you to be more concise. You'll be able to cut out extraneous words and phrases and have an easy response when people ask you the inevitable question of "What does your firm do?" or "What do you do?"

- When meeting someone for the first time, try to find a personal interest. Personal interests help people feel more connected, and they provide starting points for subsequent conversations. Tell them what you know about them or their company and offer sincere compliments about what you may know about them or projects that company has done.

- As soon as you have an opportunity, make a note on the back of his or her card. When you return to the office, add the name to your contacts manager and record any information that might prove helpful later. Follow up to set up a meeting or send additional information. Send a "nice to meet you" e-mail note as soon as possible and attach your list of professional capabilities or a link to your website. Make it easy for him or her to learn more about your firm. Most people will have met a lot of other people at these events and it helps to refresh their memories about your firm and its capabilities—and to connect you to the firm.

- Be seen multiple times in order to be remembered. Some groups are small and everyone knows each other. In this case, upon arrival have an idea of who you want to talk with and make it a point to locate them. Don't monopolize anyone's time; remember they are here to talk with other people, too. If more time is required, ask if you may call to set up a lunch or a time to talk outside of this event.

- During conversations, be aware of the other person's body language. Also be aware of your own body language and how you are coming across. Be confident and smile. Make this person feel as if he or she is the only person in the room that is important to you.

- Remind yourself to remember people's names—note the spelling on their name tags. Using their names a couple of times will help you to remember it. Visually connect each person with his or her name. Try to gather a bit of personal information to use next time you see that person.

- Ask a few open-ended questions in order to gather information. It's OK to *briefly* share similar experiences—but the other person should be doing most of the talking.

- Volunteer for committees and offices. It's important to participate in the organization in order to be perceived as someone worth knowing. Volunteering helps you to gain credibility and visibility. You will be viewed as a trusted peer by those that can give you work or recommend you to others. By taking a leadership role in the organization, you will also improve your own professional skills and abilities.

- A networking event is not about the lunch or even the presentations, so don't focus on the content. The presentation or the speaker is just a way to draw people to the event. The fee that is charged by the organization is to help pay for the facility and the lunch. It is a way for the association to provide the opportunity for its members to network.

- Remember to thank the event coordinators for their efforts in putting everything together.

Listening Skills. Knowing how to listen can sometimes be even more important than knowing how to speak. During conversations at a networking event, make sure your body language says you are interested and actively listening. Square your shoulders to the person speaking. Lean slightly forward and make eye contact; don't glance around the room.

Nod occasionally to show that you understand. Keep facial expressions appropriate to what is being said.

How To Approach Someone

- A person standing alone is easy to approach—just walk up, offer a handshake, and introduce yourself. The person will welcome the opportunity to reply and to have someone to talk with. Most people are shy around strangers.
- When approaching a group of people that you do not know, first wait to be recognized before interrupting. Then just smile, offer your hand to the first person that made eye contact, and say, "Hello, I'm ___"
- If someone you know is talking with another person that you do not know, approach with a smile. If they have any manners, they will introduce you. If not just introduce yourself.
- Everyone has their own style of networking, so just be you.
- Keep in mind that everyone is there for the same purpose, and so your introduction will be welcome.
- Learn to ask open-ended questions that solicit the kind of information you need in order to determine if this is someone you need to get to know better. It's not about talking a lot—actually, too much talking is a negative. It's hard to learn about another person when you are doing all the talking.

Try this role play with your friends or coworkers until you are comfortable. Learning is much easier and faster when you experience situations first hand rather than just reading about them.

Role Play: You are approaching someone at a networking event. What would you do and say in each of these situations?

1. **Single person alone (use your elevator speech)**
2. **A group**
3. **Someone you know talking to another person that you do not know**

Conversation Starters. When you meet people for the first time, learn how to ask the right open-ended questions that get people to talk about their business. Be flexible; don't just use a script, but start the conversation with some questions in mind and go with the flow. It's not about talking—you don't have to talk much at all. When the other person is doing most of the talking, they think you are so nice and so smart!

While offering your handshake, say, "Hi, I'm __ with XYZ." As the other person introduces himself or herself, there are a number of open-ended questions that can create a meaningful conversation. Keep it light at the first meeting with just a few get-acquainted inquiries. After introductions have been made, choose two or three of the following suggestions for conversation starters:

- "Joe, what is your role at the firm? How long have you been there?"
- "What do you like most about what you do?"
- "What brought you to this event?"
- You might mention someone you know at the other person's firm.
- You might ask if he or she is familiar with your firm or a specific project.
- You might bring up a recent news item or sporting event.
- "What other organizations do you belong to that are content-rich/ interesting?"
- "Who is the most interesting/funny/ knowledgeable person you have met here?"
- "How does this information relate to your firm?"

- If there is someone that you have wanted to meet, ask if he or she knows that person and would introduce you: "Would you mind introducing me?"
- You could ask about his or her target market and if there is anyone you know that you might be able to introduce him to.
- "What's new in your industry?"
- "What are some of the challenges in your business?"
- "What got you into this profession?"
- "What do you like most about your business?"

You get the idea. Above all—be yourself. Build a network of people who enjoy knowing you for who you are, not a persona that you put on for business networking.

What Should You *Not* Talk About at Networking Events? You can never be sure about the background of the people in the room or what people believe. There are always varying opinions when you get a group of people together and this is not the time for you to try to change anyone's opinion—no matter how nicely you might try. A few rules to remember:

- It is not safe to talk about politics, religion, sex, race, or any ethnic-sensitive issues. Even when someone agrees with you, comments about any of these can be easily misconstrued and do nothing to further your professional image.
- Never comment on how someone is dressed or on another person's attire (unless it's obvious that this is the purpose, such as a loud tie or a costume designed for attention).
- Talk in terms of the other person's interests. Don't spend the time talking about yourself. The more you allow the other person to talk, the better he or she will like you.

- Try to spend only five to ten minutes with each person, because there is a limited amount of networking time before the meeting begins. Thirty minutes equals talking to three to six people.
- Be selective. Obtaining answers to just a few questions, such as the person's role, will help you to determine the potential value of networking with this person. Try to gain an understanding of the firm and his or her position. If the other person's firm offers complementary services, ask how you might help or try to find an opportunity to team.
- The most important of all the rules is to follow up after the meeting and to stay in touch. If there is a secret to networking, it is in the follow-up. Send new contacts a note after the event and check their online presence through LinkedIn or Facebook.

Ending the conversation. Moving on to talk with someone else is a necessary skill to learn—otherwise you may get "stuck" with someone who is monopolizing your time with no benefit to you in return. Remember the other person is here to network as well, so be considerate of his or her time.

After you have spent five to ten minutes with this person, say something like: "Joe, it was very nice talking with you. I'll let you go now so that you can talk to some other folks, but let's stay in touch. May I call you next week to set up a time to talk more?" Shake hands and walk away. Or, you might introduce him to someone else and leave them to talk.

Move to a different area of the room before introducing yourself to someone new so that it is not obvious that you are "working the room". You might stop to say hello to someone you know on your way. This may all sound contrived, but it will become easier and feel more natural with practice.

Try this role play with your co-workers before attending the next networking event:

Practice Role Play: You are meeting someone for the first time at a networking event.

1. **Use two or three get-acquainted questions.**
2. **Practice ending the conversation.**

At a Lunch Meeting. Many trade organization meetings will be centered on a speaker presenting information of interest to the group along with a sit-down lunch. How the situation is managed can make a difference in how many new people you meet.

- Sit with people whom you have not met before, and meet everyone at your table.
- Sit with someone who is sitting alone.
- Sit with a potential client or teaming partner.
- Never sit with coworkers. Split up and cover more territory.
- Pass food items (bread, butter, salt and pepper, cream, etc.) to your left. Don't be the one that sits on the butter.
- Use good table manners. Don't talk with food in your mouth.
- Most people prefer not to shake hands when food is being consumed, so be considerate. Some do a fist bump instead of a handshake.
- Listen more than you talk, but do participate in the conversation and always take advantage of opportunities to point to your firm's capabilities without getting too sales-like.
- Offer your business card and collect business cards from everyone at your table. People are flattered when you ask for a business card. You are telling them that they are important to you and you want to remember their name and company.

- Follow up with an e-mail when you get back to the office: "Nice meeting you…Would like to get together to talk more about _____ or just to get better acquainted?"

Eating at an Event. There are mixed opinions about eating at a stand-up affair. Some feel that eating with others is an equalizing exercise—the other person feels that you are sharing with him or her. Some people feel that eating creates an awkward situation and that you should either eat before arriving at the event or after everyone has left. Do whatever feels most comfortable for you, but always with impeccable manners. Choose foods that are easy to eat without dripping. Take small bites, because you never know when someone might approach you and expect you to speak.

Here's a plate-balancing trick that might prove helpful at a stand-up event where finger food is served:

1. Hold your plate in your right hand.
2. Pick up small bites of food with your left hand.
3. When someone approaches to shake hands, switch your plate to your left hand.
4. Shake hands, and then move your plate back to your right hand.

Your left hand (the eating hand) remains free of germs and your right hand (your shaking hand) is free of food particles!

Male/Female Etiquette. There is a general uncertainty about the proper place for gender-related manners in business. While it is always proper to be respectful of the other person, the special courtesies that men give to women in a social setting are not required in business. It is OK for a man to offer a handshake to a woman first in a business setting. It is OK for a woman to open the door for a man if she arrives first. Let everyone open their own car doors. It's always nice to be courteous to others, but keep in mind this is business—not a date.

Networking with Peers. Personal or peer networking is a little different, but is very important, too. It's about people helping each other. It's personal. It's like a checking account—you must make deposits in order to be able to make withdrawals. Always be on the lookout for ways to help others; it will come back to you—if not from that person then it will come from someone else.

How do you feel when someone helps you? Don't you want to help in return? Of course; that's how it works. Spend the time to get to know people in order to learn how you can help them, and let them know how they can help you, too. Get to know people so well that you know their hobbies and interests and their personal priorities. Know their business challenges and goals. When you do, you will always have something to talk about with them. It gives you a reason to stay in touch.

Ask people questions about themselves and volunteer to help. Move out of your own head about what to say and how to sound engaging, and just turn it around. Be interested in the other person's perspective, career, and interests, and the conversation will flow. You will build a relationship based on reciprocation. Always end conversations by asking, "What can I do to help you? Is there anyone you think I should know? Would you make an introduction?"

This is not too forward. How would you feel if someone asked you to introduce him or her to someone you felt they should know? You would be happy to help make such a connection. That's great networking!

When networking with peers, the emphasis should be on fostering relationships throughout your career. A network of peers can be useful for conducting informal market research, getting a feel for a changing market, keeping up with trends in the industry, gathering information about the competitors, checking out rumors, or getting an early lead on potential project opportunities. To be considered a valuable member of a network, you must also share information. When you do share information with others, do so in such a way as to not give away company secrets.

Be selective about where and to whom you will give information. Increase your value by sharing the most valuable information with only a few people that have the potential to help you the most. It helps to anchor the networking relationship with them.

When building your personal network, seek out people from diverse backgrounds. You never know who people know or who might give you a great referral. People outside of your industry who have no knowledge of it can be good resources for referrals.

Call peers occasionally and ask what's going on. Check on their families or invite them to lunch. Everyone has to eat, so it might as well be productive time. It provides an opportunity for you to discuss how well your business is doing, exchange thoughts and general information, and uncover potentially great teaming opportunities. Try to plan a networking lunch at least once a week.

The primary rule of most effective networking with peers is staying in touch. Never lose contact with a networking friend. If a friend gets a new job, send a congratulatory note. A new baby or a new house or any life event provides an opportunity to make contact and to stay in touch.

Networking with people that you know can not only generate leads from them, but can also generate leads from the people that they know. A good way to get started is to make a list of everyone you know:

- *Existing clients*—those that you are in constant contact with
- *Previous clients*—those that you've worked with before, going back ten years
- *Vendors* can help keep you in the know about who is doing what.
- *People you went to school with* may now be working at a company that could give you work, or they might become good teaming partners.
- *People you knew at previous jobs.*

Your networking target list of peers should be constantly evolving; you'll be making additions or changes as you meet new people. Make a list; you will be amazed at how many people you do know!

Finding the time to network with peers or new contacts can be a management challenge. Setting aside a few minutes at a certain time of day is most effective. Fifteen minutes first thing in the morning every day to make a few calls (before getting into e-mails) can make a significant impact on your business growth.

Social Situations. A good way to build relationships with potential networking friends or potential clients is while attending social situations. At social events, people tend to be more relaxed and receptive to interaction with people that they do not know. Such events provide great opportunities to get to know people on a personal level.

- At social events it is usually best to keep your interactions light and then follow up later to set up a meeting to discuss business details.
- At sporting events, there are several theories about discussing business. For instance, on the golf course, most people like to concentrate on their game, so wait for the client or potential client to take the lead. At some point the other person will ask what you or your firm does, and then you can give a brief summary of your firm's services.

- Be sensitive to the other person's level of interest. If he or she does not appear interested, drop it or bring up another area that might apply more to the other person's area of responsibility.
- Save the heavy stuff for later…and there really is never a good time to get salesy or pushy during a social event.
- During the social time after the game you can ask questions to direct the conversation that will allow you to find new business opportunities.
- Holidays and special events present an excellent opportunity to network. Begin early in the season by accepting every invitation, even if it's not the perfect venue. You never know who you will meet.
- Whatever the event, keep in mind that you are representing the company. Conduct yourself, and your Business Development efforts, so that they reflect your company's values and ethics. Honesty, good manners, and personal consideration of others will always be required.

Conferences and Tradeshows. Working a tradeshow or conference is a specialty in itself. If done correctly it is very hard work, both mentally and physically. Tradeshow participation is typically more about meeting lots of people than it is about obtaining leads. Success can sometimes be difficult to immediately measure because the people you meet will need further nurturing before they become clients.

- Decide if it is worth the cost and your time to attend. Keep in mind that "costly" does not necessarily mean it is better for your business. Some of the best shows for your business may cost very little.
  - o Will your target prospects or existing clients be attending?
  - o Conduct research of your own. Don't rely on promotions for the show. Tradeshows are managed and promoted by third parties who stand to gain profit based on the number of attendees.

- o Talk to past attendees to determine if they found the event to be of value.
- o Check out the speakers to see how relevant their subjects are and how much industry experience they have.
- o Check out who is exhibiting. Will the big companies be there? Are your competitors going to be there?

- If you decide to participate, look for sponsorship opportunities. Money spent on sponsorships will pay off more than trinkets or give-a ways. Give-a-ways must be high quality or they can do more harm than good for the company's image.
  - o You might be able team up with one of your suppliers to share the cost.
  - o Sponsors generally receive free passes as part of their package. You can give them to clients or prospects.

- Start before the conference. Your job begins long before you arrive at the conference.
  - o Obtain a list of people that have registered.
  - o Ask your marketing department to send out announce-ment cards to clients and prospective clients letting them know you will be there.
    - Announcement cards help to open the intro-duction.
    - They also help with image building and creat-ing name recognition.

- Preplan the event so that you know who you're going to talk to before you get there.
  - o Choose several new contacts that you want to meet from the registered attendees list. Consider asking someone to help you find them and to introduce you.

- o Make a point to locate and talk with people you have met before. If after a brief hello and initial discussion you find it necessary to have an extended conversations, book appointment times to talk with them.
- o Never monopolize a person's time without permission. Other people are there to network also, and will avoid you if they feel you take too much of their time every time they run into you.
- o Spending quality time with ten to fifteen of the right people each day is reasonable. How many you choose to have on your list will depend on the length of the tradeshow and the attendees.

- Attend the welcome reception before the event begins and all end of the day cocktail receptions sponsored by vendors.
  - o Alcohol consumption should be minimized. You want to be able to think clearly and to take advantage of opportunities to talk about your company's capabilities. In addition, you will want to able to remember the conversation and a person's name the next day.
- While waiting in a line, talk to people standing in front of and behind you. You never know who they might be. Don't be pushy— just friendly.
- Always wear your name badge. The visual image makes it easier for others to associate your face with your name and your company and to remember it.
- If you have an exhibit booth:
  - o Create a work schedule so that you are not spending all your time standing in the booth waiting for them to come to you….Go out and find them.

- o Many people never enter the exhibit hall, but you can locate them at the sessions or around the common areas.
- Arrange to take clients to dinner, but also make an effort to have dinner with someone you do not know that might be a good networking contact or potential client. Just ask—most people are flattered by an invitation even if they have made prior plans.
- Make an effort to speak to those you already know, but most of your focus should be on speaking to new people.
- Remember to not sell at the conference, it's best to work toward setting up an appointment for a later date to discuss ways to be of service.
  - o If someone mentions a specific project, get a few details in order to provide information, but save the heavy exchange of information for outside of the event.
- Free yourself from office and other responsibilities.
  - o Your time at conferences is important time and is costing the company money, so focus on what you need to be doing.
  - o Post an "out of office" message on your e-mail and check phone messages at the end of the day. Assign someone to call you in case of emergency and plan to only answer that person's call.
  - o Wear comfortable shoes and soft socks—your feet will thank you. Conference floors are concrete, so it might help to wear soft insoles in your shoes. Ladies, don't wear high heels. You can always tell the novice tradeshow attendees by the choice of shoes.
- You may choose to not waste time on the meals at a tradeshow because most of the food is costly and bad anyway.
  - o The only reason to stop for lunch is that it presents an opportunity to meet a prospect.

- o Bring along a couple of snacks and use the extra time to make contacts.
- Don't forget business cards. It seems you always need more than you think you will.
- Attend sessions that are relevant to your business. One of the other attendees just may be someone you've wanted to meet, or may be someone who needs the services your company provides.
  - o If the session is not a good fit or is not presented well, don't worry about how it looks if you leave—this is your time and money.
  - o Share information gathered at sessions with other staff members. Make handouts of what you learned that might benefit others in the company.
  - o If several of you are attending the same event, you may want to plan to split up and cover more territory.
- Don't allow anyone to consume your time that is not worthwhile. Choose where you will be and use your time wisely.
- When you get back to the office, don't just file everything away.
  - o Follow up again with new contacts to let them know you enjoyed meeting them.
  - o Try to set up another meeting, especially if there is a project coming up.
  - o Keep them on your schedule for continuous follow-up with an article or some piece of information of interest.
  - o Circulate the materials you collected to others in the group who might have an interest.
- Experience says that it generally takes about nine contacts with someone before they begin to take you seriously. E-mails and phone calls all count and are OK, but face-to-face meetings work much better.

Becoming a successful networker takes time, commitment, persistence, and patience. You must be willing to *give* first. Mastery of the skill of networking will result in you being seen as a leader and will create more business opportunities for your company. The important thing to remember about networking and tradeshows is that you have to be where people are and find a way to interact with them in any way that you feel comfortable.

Networking is about:

- becoming known by those that can help you in business
- creating momentum toward achieving business and career success
- turning social contacts into clients and friends
- building and nurturing long-term relationships
- building a people-resource bank that pays dividends and will compound annually for life

When it comes to networking, plan on getting out of it what you put into it. Sometimes 80 percent of success is just showing up—that's particularly true for networking. Put it on your calendar and make it a priority. Be enthusiastic and enjoy the process!

Rules for Networking

<u>**Do**</u>

1. Put cell phone on silent or vibrate and keep it out of sight.
2. Be seen multiple times in order to be remembered.
3. Look and act professionally at all times.
4. Focus all of your attention on the person in front of you. Listen attentively. Square your shoulders to his or hers and make eye contact.
5. Ask the right questions so that you are listening more than talking.
6. Be aware of body language—both yours and theirs.

7. Remember names and use them.

8. Be upbeat and positive. Be enthusiastic. Enjoy meeting new people (they will know if you don't).

9. Participate and become actively involved in the organization: take an office, or lead a committee.

10. Try to sit next to people that you do *not* already know.

11. Get a business card from everyone at your table—and give them yours.

12. Follow up:

    a. As soon as you return to the office, add new contacts to your database, add notes, and schedule any follow-up activities required.

    b. Send a "nice to meet you" note to new contacts as soon as you return to the office. You might attach a "list of services" sheet and direct them to your website. Your contacts will be meeting lots of other people, and your follow-up helps them remember you and connect you with your company.

    c. Remember to follow up. It usually takes six to nine contacts before anything happens. Types of contact might be:

        1. phone calls—always leave a voice message
        2. handwritten notes—congratulations on life events
        3. e-mails—avoid forwarding
        4. meet again at networking events
        5. send news or technical article of interest or project write-ups of interest

13. Remember that peer networking is a two-way street. You must be willing to give in order to be able to ask for help when you need it.

14. Make networking work for you—have fun with it!

<u>Don't</u>

1. Don't talk on your cell phone during networking time. If you *must* take a call, do so out of sight. It is bad manners to check messages or e-mail during the presentation or while someone is speaking.
2. Don't check your phone when others might want to talk to you. It could be viewed as a screen—to keep others from talking to you.
3. Don't hang out or sit with coworkers.
4. Don't make personal comments about hair, clothes, etc.
5. Don't talk politics or religion or any other sensitive issue.
6. Don't talk about yourself unless asked (except to *briefly* share similar experiences).
7. Don't survey the room to see who else you want to talk to while speaking with someone.
8. Don't talk badly about the competition, repeat gossip, or make negative comments.
9. Don't be argumentative or take an opposite stand.
10. Don't be salesy or pushy. Instead, try to make a personal connection. Offer information about your firm's capabilities, ask the right open-ended questions, and set another time to meet to discuss a particular project.

<u>Key Concepts in this Chapter</u>

1. Networking can be one of the most efficient Business Development tools for a small company.
2. Interacting with people at networking events creates visibility and credibility for your firm. It can make it easy to meet prospective clients, to learn industry trends, and find out what competitors are doing.
3. There are many different types of networking. Each type should be worked differently and will provide different benefits.

4. This chapter includes role play ideas and conversation starters that can be practiced with coworkers.

5. The more effective you can work a networking event, the more successful you will be at uncovering leads for new business.

7

USING THE TELEPHONE

The telephone can be an indispensable tool for growing your business. Make it work for *you*—think of it as your friend and don't be intimidated by it. We are not talking about using the phone to make a bunch of cold calls one after the other. That seldom works and is not very productive. When you have a clearly defined target and know what you need to say, then a telephone call can be powerful and can be used to create all kinds of beginnings. The Business Development process is just a series of building blocks, and the telephone will get you quickly to that first step in the process. A few minutes on the phone each day, making calls to new prospects and existing clients, can make a tremendous difference in your business.

As a business tool, there are endless ways the telephone can be used. A few of those could be to:

- initiate contact with a person that you wish to meet
- introduce yourself and your company's capabilities
- further a relationship with someone that you recently met at a networking event
- make an appointment to meet

- research and gather information about future needs of your existing clients
- make contacts with prospective new clients
- develop an existing relationship further
- gain credibility and trust
- follow up on new leads
- confirm activities related to proposals
- address a project issue or problem

Doing business by phone comes with its own set of challenges. For professional service providers it can be really tough to feel good about stopping billable work to make phone calls. The following pointers may help to make the process easier and more time efficient.

Get Organized and Plan. Before you start making calls, know who you will call and why. It is easier to get started making calls when you pull everything together before you ever dial a number. There are four basic preparation steps that apply to almost any situation.

1. **Find the Right Person**. Maybe you have a name from a networking event, but is he or she the right person? Finding the right person is the key to having success using the telephone. You might check the company website for an organization chart or a list of executives. The Contact Us or Careers pages can also give you a clue. If you're not sure if you have the right person, ask whoever answers the phone or press "0" and go back to the receptionist. When you call an individual, it's OK to ask if he or she is the right person. If the person you have reached is not, then he or she will tell who you need to talk with. The higher in the organization you reach, the more likely you are to get directed to the right person. In addition, you will have a higher-up person's name to drop when you do reach the person you need.

2. **Set Up a Meeting**. The telephone is the logical tool to use for setting up a meeting with someone you may have met briefly or may not know at all. A face-to-face meeting provides so much more than only a telephone conversation can do because you can see body language and expressions. Keep in mind that too much conversation during the first phone call actually makes it more difficult to set up a meeting. If you give too much information or answer all of his or her questions, then the person will see no need to set up a meeting with you. So, keep your conversation short, but long enough to gain your contact's interest.

3. **Why Are You Calling?** When thinking about the conversation you will have, know what you are going to say and what information you need. Have a clear understanding of why you're making the call, and don't dial until you can clearly articulate what you want to say. Your call is a good time to ask open-ended questions and allow the other person to tell you his or her issues and concerns.

4. **Prepare Open-Ended Questions Ahead**. From your previous research, you may have gathered an understanding of the company and a strategic appreciation for the issues that the prospect's industry in general might be facing. Ask about those issues using open-ended question. Do not make assumptions about anything—let the other person tell you. Try asking it something like this: "I'm hearing about (whatever the issue is) that the industry is facing. In what way will the issue affect your company?" Check the company website for anything else that might be a conversation starter. Look for news items, the types of projects they do, and any possible issues and concerns. Use preplanned questions in a natural way. The more prepared you are, the more comfortable you (and your prospect) will feel.

5. **Check Your Mind-Set**. Make sure your thoughts are positive and upbeat and that you have a good outcome in mind. Your mind-set is the way you see yourself, so make sure you are having positive self-

image thoughts such as "I am a highly regarded professional" or "I am an expert that they will come to respect once they know me." See yourself as a trusted helper—a provider of a solution to a problem. At this point you are not *selling* anything.

The Introduction. Be very clear and concise when introducing yourself and your business. This is where you position yourself and your purpose. State who you are and the purpose of your call. You may want to rehearse a few phrases of explanation to get you started. Write them down and practice until it comes easily and naturally. Use your elevator speech, but be flexible to the situation. There is no magic script because every situation is different.

When you identify yourself, give your full name, your function, and your company. If your name or your company is unusual, you may want to spell it out. Make sure you speak slowly and clearly. If the other person has to try to figure out what you just said or who you are, it detracts from the purpose of your call. Example: "Good morning, Mr. Smith. This is John Young. I am the operations manager for XYZ Company and I'm calling to follow up with you about..." or, "I would like to talk with you about..." Then go into the purpose of the call. Always approach it from how it benefits the other person. That's really what he or she is listening to hear.

Show respect for the contact's time. When the person answers the phone, first ask if he or she has a minute: "Is this a good time to talk?" If the other person says this really is a bad time, then ask when it would be OK for you to call back.

It helps to reference someone in common when possible. "I received your name from Mary Smith at ABC Company." Or you might say that Mary Smith referred you to him or her as the right person. This works very well if Mary Smith is a superior. In your initial conversation, it is

OK to ask the other person's area of responsibility. Listen for his or her needs and concerns, and remember that this person should be doing 70 percent of the talking. You just politely ask the questions that direct the conversation.

Following a brief introduction and a statement of your purpose; ask two to three open-ended questions to gain the information you need. An open-ended question might be something like "How did you enjoy the conference?" or "What is your firm planning to do about…?" Such a question can invite a wide range of responses. The response you receive will give you an idea of what's important to this person and what's on his or her mind. Sincerely asked open-ended questions can begin any number of conversations.

Keep the first phone call to about three to five minutes, unless the prospect obviously wants to talk further. It is best to save in-depth conversation for the first meeting, which you will schedule as you are talking and before the interest is gone. Always thank the other person for his or her time as you say good-bye.

First Impression. Use the first phone call to create interest in your company's services and to establish a personal connection with an identified target. It is the first impression you will make. You have about thirty seconds to create a positive first impression and to establish the beginnings of trust. The first phone call helps to begin the rapport-building process with a prospective client and sets up the opportunity for further discussion. Use your phone to gather information that helps create value by offering specific solutions to problems your client or prospect might have.

Talk with the person. *Visualize* the person you are calling, even if you don't know him or her yet. Check for information on LinkedIn or other media sites, and you will likely see a photo and other relevant information about the person that might prove helpful. Remind yourself you are engaged in a two-way conversation with a human and not with a phone. Try to connect with the individual. Always be professional, natural, open, honest, and straightforward. Don't be multi-tasking while on the phone, it's just rude and is obvious to the other person. Take notes and use them at the end of your conversation to confirm your understanding and to let the other person know you paid attention.

When having a conversation on the phone with a prospect, ask the right questions that let you know what concerns he or she faces. Listen actively and make sure you talk less than the prospect does. Don't be in a rush— but get to the point quickly as to why you have called. Respect the other person's time, but don't be put off by it. Times is valuable to everyone, but remember you are providing value and will become an important part of the other person's success in the future.

Think in terms of the acronym **S.A.L.E.** You must:

1. **Stop** talking (selling) and listen more.
2. **Ask** if this is a good time (it gives you permission).
3. **Listen** carefully and make notes.
4. **Empathize** (or educate) and let the other person know you care.

Manage Expectations. Expect a good outcome of the call—something you enjoy doing. It's really not that difficult to use the telephone as a Business Development tool when you make it a daily habit and see it as an enjoyable time to connect with customers. It seems that the most difficult thing for some people is dialing the number. Once they get started, they wonder why the task seemed so difficult to do. Manage how you allow your mind to think about this important part of your job.

The question on the other end is always going to be: "Why are you calling me and why should I take the time listen to you?" If you can articulate the answer to that in such a way that the other person sees the benefit from his or her perspective, you will quickly gain credibility. If you can be clear on this for yourself, it will give you more confidence. Keep in mind that the prospect needs you; he or she just may not know it yet.

Schedule Phone Time. When using the phone as a Business Development tool to find new leads or to follow up, it works best to schedule your phone time. Write it down; it's amazing how much easier it is to get something done when it is written down and scheduled. Use an electronic task manager, or make an entry on your calendar with the person's name and phone number included. Having all the information together saves time and makes it easier to get started because you don't have to waste time searching for the information you need. The important thing is to do it every day.

If you have other responsibilities, make it a habit to spend just ten to fifteen minutes of phone time each day, and you will see amazing results. Enter the time as an appointment on your calendar that must be kept. If your business is new or struggling and you desperately need business, you may want to schedule additional phone time. Enter the phone numbers into your phone for those people that you may be calling often, so that the numbers are quick and easy to locate. If you tend to put off making phone calls, it might help to make a short call to a friend first just to get you started. Keep it brief. In a business setting, the phone is not for long social conversations or idle chit-chat. Time is too valuable. Apply your time where it will gain you and your business the most benefit.

Ending the Call. It's one thing to know how to make calls and how to have a productive conversation, but what about ending the call in a positive way? You always want to leave the other person feeling that the call has been worthwhile and that you care about his or her situation. When you feel that you have covered all that needs to be said, then simply say something like, "John, thank you for talking with me. I know you are busy, so I will let you go." Remember it is all about other people and their needs. You might want to confirm a couple of key points of the conversation and what you see as the next step. Have a clear understanding of what actions are needed before the next call or meeting, and try to set the stage for that while you have the person on the phone.

Let the other person know when you will get back with him or her. If there is not a particular reason to call back again, ask if it is OK to touch base periodically just to see how things are going. If you had a good reason to call in the first place—even if just to introduce yourself—he or she will not refuse the offer. This way the other person is giving you permission to call again. The last thirty seconds of a call can be just as important as the first thirty seconds. How you end the call leaves a lasting impression and will determine how the listener will finalize his or her opinion of you. Be professional, positive, and upbeat, and always be thinking about what the next step will be.

Reasons to Call. There are many reasons to call a prospect or client. You just have to give it some thought. There are holidays, special events, news items, follow-up from having met at a networking event or tradeshow—lots of reasons. Keep a running list of people you want to call and work from it each day. If you have a phone with task reminder capabilities, you can quickly remind yourself of a name you wish to add to your list even while on the go. There are many reasons to call existing and prospective clients. You can always call just to see how things are going—everyone likes to feel that others care. Try to know ahead of time what their issues *might* be. Check their website for new postings. You might even want to keep a file of interesting items to discuss.

Plan your discussion as much as possible before dialing, but allow for flexibility because you never know how people might need your service. Show value—be able to articulate how you can be of service. Have an idea of the expected outcome of the call you are about to make.

Some examples of good reasons to call would be:

1. introducing your business for the first time
2. setting an appointment to meet and explore how you can be of support
3. recognizing or congratulating about a special event, award, or news item
4. asking this person to introduce you to the decision-maker
5. opening a dialogue for further discussion
6. following up from a previous encounter (possibly a networking event)
7. trying to identify the right person in another business—to get a referral
8. other possible phone call goals with existing clients
   a. discussing a particular upcoming project
   b. introducing additional services
   c. gaining introductions to other divisions
   d. resolving an issue or concern
   e. holiday wishes
   f. life event congratulations: wedding, birthday, new house, new baby

Additional Tips:

Use Props. Gather all your information in front of you before you make the call so you can refer to it as you talk on the phone. This is one of the good things about talking on the phone versus in person. You can have as many props as you need, and nobody needs to know.

Focus. When you make your calls, make sure your space is free of noise and distractions and focus on what you are doing. Put away everything that does not relate to this call. If you try to multitask, you will not be focused on the call and the listener will know it. Listen attentively and ask thought provoking, open-ended questions that show you understand his or her situation.

Relax. Be genuine—just relax and be yourself when talking on the phone. A relaxed posture tends to create a relaxed approach, so get comfortable. Use a good chair, or better yet stand up. Show interest in the other person by asking questions that help you learn about him or her. Keep in mind that people like to do business with people they like and that they feel like them in return. That's the beginning of trust.

Smile. Your listener can feel it. Smile and be polite and considerate, but not tentative. Be strong and confident, but not arrogant. It might help to stand while talking on the phone. Standing expands your lungs and makes your voice stronger. The vocal and verbal message you communicate on the phone needs to match your nonverbal message, even if it cannot be seen. The best way to improve your skills and gain confidence is to record yourself and notice what might be a distraction or would send a less favorable impression. Pay attention to your body language and gestures, and make sure they are positive because they come across as you speak. Your listener can hear the difference. What you do on your end of the phone when you smile and have positive thoughts will come across to your listener as strong and confident.

Breathe. Before you pick up the phone, take a deep breath to relax. As the other person answers, take a breath and begin speaking on the exhale. The listener will hear energy in your voice. Most of us are shallow breathers, especially at the office. We take in small breaths and our voice comes across as tired and small. The goal is to sound as if you love this job and your company, and you are excited to share information with this person.

Getting Around Obstacles. There will always be obstacles but in order to be successful using the telephone we must be politely persistent. Remind yourself that this person needs your service. If you continue to have trouble getting through, try calling during lunch in the person's time zone or after hours. The other person may reach for the phone without thinking. Most people have caller ID and can see who is calling, so you might try calling from a cell phone or home phone or a different phone. This is not trickery—you are just being resourceful about how you reach an individual. If you have determined that the person or company you are calling could benefit from your service but the individual you are trying to reach keeps putting you off, or is rude, consider that you may have the wrong person. Start over and conduct additional research to locate the right person.

Getting Past the Palace Guard. Gatekeepers can block you from the person you want to speak with. Try asking for their help. Everyone likes to help, especially good administrative professionals. Ask the gatekeeper if he or she manages the schedule of the person you're trying to reach, or if he or she can help you get a message to that person. If it is obvious the gatekeeper is not willing to help you, there are many tactics for bypassing him or her. Try calling when the gatekeeper is not there. Early mornings or late evenings can be a good time to catch executives. Administrative people tend to keep regular hours, but busy executives seldom do. Get thru to anybody and ask to be transferred.

Match His or Her Speech. Speak at a moderately fast pace. Match your volume and rate of speech to your listener. If the other person speaks slowly, then you speak slowly. If the other person is a fast talker, then speed your speech up. Generally it is best to speak just a notch faster than the other person—unless, of course, he or she speaks very fast; then it might get silly. Speaking too quickly may give the impression that you are rushing to get off the phone or trying to push. The opposite, speaking too slowly, can make you sound less credible or cause the listener to lose interest. The more considerate you are of your listener, the more professional you will sound.

Articulate Clearly. Be able to articulate your message clearly. Pronunciation and enunciation are amplified over the phone. Avoid annoying speech patterns and repetitive phrases. Stammering and repeating yourself until you find what you are trying to say can send a negative impression. Avoid the "ums" and "ahs" in your speech patterns. Take time to listen to yourself and clean up your act before subjecting your listeners to them.

Don't Use the Phone Speaker. Consider using a headset in order to keep your hands free and never use the speaker unless absolutely necessary. It creates a concern that someone other than you can hear what is being said. If you are in a situation that requires using the speaker, let the other person know who else is in the room and assure him or her that the office door is closed.

It Is Personal. This may be a business call but when it really comes down to it, it's all personal, so be sure to address the listener by name more frequently than you would in face-to-face conversations. Everyone likes to hear their name, and this conveys to the listener that you are fully present in the conversation. Perceptions are inflated when there are no visual communication aids, so addressing your listener by name sends a favorable impression. Using his or her name creates the visualization of a connection. Know how to pronounce it properly and use it often. People tend to like you better when they hear you say their name often. In many scenarios you can call their office and ask the receptionist how to pronounce the name before you call the prospect's personal line. Do your homework on the prospect and their company. Let the prospect know you've done your due diligence.

Find a Connection. Try to find a personal connection with your prospects. Offer commonalities of interest. Do you have children the same age? Do you enjoy the same types of sports? Show them that you care. Differentiate yourself by going the extra mile. For a professional services business that requires a long-term relationship, you must first be their friend, and really want to help them. You are not just trying to sell them something. Be genuine and not contrived. This will go a long way toward assuring a return call, gaining their trust, and eventually winning their business.

The "Commercial" Phone Message. Most of the time when making business calls, you will get voice mail, so be prepared to leave a message. This is good because now you have the opportunity to leave your commercial. During your commercial, speak slowly and clearly. Your message must be very concise and compelling. Make it interesting but short and upbeat, to the point, memorable, and persuasive. You have to be able to point out the benefit that will cause the other person to want to call you back. It's best to not provide all the details at this point. Leave something for the imagination, and speak with enthusiasm. You can't expect your prospect to be excited about calling you back if you're not excited. So be animated and don't speak in a monotone voice. Your prospects will often mirror your emotions, so concentrate on being positive without sounding phony. Make sure your confidence and belief in what you are offering shine through. At this point you are focused on getting this person to return your call.

Leave just enough information to gain the prospect's interest, but make sure it's not an empty promise. When people call back, you don't want them to feel as if they've been tricked. You might say something like, "I have some information that I think will be of interest to you." Intrigue them, make them curious, and leave them wanting more information.

In some types of business, it helps to offer an incentive. If you are offering an incentive, be sure to repeat it at least twice during the message. Mention it once near the beginning, and again at the end so it's fresh in the listener's mind. Your objective is to get the other person to call back, and if it takes a little bribery, then so be it. Be creative and sincere, and make sure your integrity is worn on your sleeve. Keep in mind that a professional services business is based on long-term lasting relationships. Treat people as you would like to be treated.

If you are offering a specific benefit, be sure to say so. Here are some ideas for general phrases that someone at a consulting firm might leave to request a meeting:

- "I would like to schedule an appointment to learn more about (the other person's firm) and see how my firm might be of support."
- "I would like to meet with you to discuss how we can be of benefit to you and your company on the XYZ project."
- Suggest a time to meet: "I plan to be in the area next week and would like to stop by to introduce myself and learn more about _____. Would you have some time available Monday or Tuesday?"

Be sure to *ask* the other person to call you back. Never assume the person understands that you want him or her to call you. It helps to create a sense of urgency. You might try, "I am in the office today and have some time and I would appreciate it if you would please give me a call back today." Leave your number twice at the end.

Send an E-mail. Try leaving your "commercial message" at two or three times different times. If there is still no response, then try this idea. At the end of your message, tell the prospect you are also going to send an e-mail with important information included, and that you will follow up. Some people find an e-mail easier to respond to and it is less intrusive to their schedule. In your e-mail, be sure the subject line connects with the message you just left. Avoid any words that might cause spam to kick it out. Keep the e-mail body simple. You could say something like:

- "This is a follow-up to my voice message this morning"
- "I would like to schedule an appointment."
- "I want to discuss XYZ project."

Along with any additional information in the body of the e-mail, you might want to attach your company fact sheet or direct the recipient to your website, or both. Make sure your phone number is easy to find on any of the information you include. Make it easy for them to call you back.

If you don't have an e-mail address, try this. Press "0" to get back to the receptionist and say, "I'm trying to send Joe some information; do you have his e-mail address?" You might also check the website on the Contact Us page, or the Careers or Officers page, to get an idea of how the company's e-mail addresses are structured. If you are speaking with anyone at the company, you might say, "I have Mr. Smith's e-mail as <u>john.smith@XYZ.com</u>; is that correct?" If not, the person will give you the proper address. It just appears that you have mistakenly written down the address that was previously given to you.

Persistence Pays Off. Professional persistence is the key to successful Business Development. This is particularly true for phone calls. Plan to call two to four times, a few days apart, and send the e-mail twice. If there is still no response, leave it alone…for a while. Add it to your schedule to try again next month and then repeat the process. Some people are busy, preoccupied, or may be out of town. It's important to not give up too soon. In most professional service firms, eighty percent of success occurs after the *ninth* contact!

Make at least nine contacts before giving up. What counts as a contact?

   (A) phone calls

   (B) voice messages

   (C) meeting at a networking event

   (D) mailings

   (E) articles, press releases, newsletters

   (F) e-mails

   (G) face-to-face meetings

   (H) follow-up calls (just to check in—it shows interest)

The next time you have a successful call ask yourself when and why that particular conversation took place. Was it after the point where you had almost given up? Many times it is.

Handling Rejection. It's going to happen, but nobody dies from it. You are sure to run into some rejections during your phone call efforts. If not, then you are probably not making enough phone calls. When you get a rejection, remember that the other person is not rejecting you personally. He or she is rejecting something else. It may be a previous experience with your company. It may be that the person does not want to deal with company contract changes and so will just settle for what he or she has currently. Or the other person may just be having a bad day. Don't take it personally and never apologize for bothering him or her. However, even if people reject you, always be gracious and thank them for their time. Remember you are a professional offering your services, and you never know when the situation might change.

When someone says, "Just send me something," and there has been very little dialogue up to this point, answer with, "I'll be glad to do that. We like to tailor our materials to meet your specific needs; is there a particular area of interest we could focus on for you?" You could then proceed to ask a question or two around the answer.

Keep in mind that any time you send information to someone, the value is in the follow-up—not in the materials you send. Call in a few days to make sure the person received it. Did it meet his or her requirements? Are there any questions? Call the contact again in a month or so and start the process over again. Sometimes people need time to make the decision to see you. As long as you are providing value, you are not a pest.

Best Time to Make Phone Calls. When is the best day of the week to schedule phone work? Whenever you do it! Some say that *Thursday* is the best day of the week to reach people. But it's more important to get it done rather than worry about which day is perfect. Mondays or Tuesdays are good because people are fresh from the weekend and not completely stressed out yet, and so they might be more open to talking with you. Friday afternoon is generally the worst time to call because most people are headed out the door—either mentally or physically. If people travel in their business, then it might be easier to catch them on Monday or Friday.

When is the best time of the day to call? Statistics show that early morning between 8:00 and 9:00 are the best times to call. At that time it is generally easier to reach people, and their minds are fresh. Another good time is late afternoon from 4:00 to 5:00, when people are wrapping up the day and organizing for the next day. But making time for phone calls is like making time for exercise—just get it done. Don't worry about the perfect day, time, or situation.

Resolving Conflict. Conflicts are always better resolved face-to-face, but if you find it necessary to use the phone to resolve a problem concerning a project, be prepared for anything before you make the call. When you reach the client, say something like, "I understand *we* have an issue", and then let the person vent first before trying to solve the problem. Sometimes people just want to know that someone cares when they are upset. Actively acknowledging another's experience does not mean that you agree or approve. Just give the other person time to feel whatever he or she feels, and then deal with the facts.

When you feel the person has completed his or her download, your response requires that you be very clear on capturing the details of the problem. People are much more likely to listen when they know they have been listened to with actively expressed acknowledgments. Talk about the issues and how they will be resolved, and who is taking care of the situation. Be able to tell the client when the problem will be resolved, and that you will follow up with him or her on how and when it is resolved. Make sure everyone is clear on the next step. Focusing on the positive outcome turns the negative into a positive and shows respect to the other person for his or her concerns.

Cell Phone Use

While we're on the subject of using the telephone as a tool, let's talk about cell phone usage. The cell phone has become an indispensable business tool. However, the way it is used can also send a negative impression to those you are calling or to people around you. When used inappropriately in a workplace setting, a cell phone conversation can easily distract or offend.

The following are some tips for making sure your use of the cell phone does not offend others or distract from your professional image.

Personal Territory. In a business situation, calling a prospect on his or her cell phone is still considered personal territory. It should only be used if you have permission or if you know this is the only phone the prospect has. Keep this in mind when you hand out your own business cards. If it is OK for people to call you on your cell, circle the number and make a point to tell them it's OK to use it.

Standardize the Ringtone. To project an image of maturity and professionalism in your business, stick with a grown-up standard ringtone rather than something funny or less professional.

Coverage Disruption. Today cell coverage is very good, but if you're taking a business call in an area that may have spotty service, let the other party know as a courtesy. That way he or she won't be surprised if there are strange background noises or if the call gets dropped, or if you get distracted by a texting pedestrian who steps into your path. Buildings with metal roofs can also disrupt cell service, so just be aware of where you are calling from and alert the other person.

Turn It Off. In a meeting, you absolutely must turn your phone off or put it on a low volume or vibrate. Colleagues and clients expect your full attention, and when you reach for your phone to check it—or worse, to answer it—you're sending the wrong message. This also applies to reviewing and answering e-mails on your phone. That's annoying and rude to others in the meeting, especially to the speaker. While the speaker may not be able to see you if you hide the phone under the table, those around you can see and it diminishes your respectability.

A scheduled meeting is not the time for cell phone calls or checking e-mails. The message you convey to those at the meeting is that they are less important than the disembodied voice coming through the cell. Unless your intention is to make others around you feel insignificant, then don't answer—turn it off, and put it out of sight. Be present and aware of the people you are with physically. Just because you have a message does not mean you have to interrupt life to respond right now. You may see some people do this and it is obvious they have a need to look important, but it sends a very negative message.

Nobody is so important that they cannot turn off their cell phone at times. If you're worried about how the office is running in your absence, check in before you start your meeting. Tell your staff that you'll be unreachable for a short while. Then hit the *off* button. The one exception to this rule might be if you're expecting a call from a doctor. Explain to the others present that you're waiting for a call about a medical emergency. If the phone rings, leave the room even before answering. Try to create the least amount of disturbance to others as possible.

Today we have texting capabilities for short messages. Consider whether the phone call is really necessary in the first place, especially if other people are nearby. We've all heard those inconsiderate types who start dialing the minute the plane lands and loudly announce, "We've just landed and I'm waiting to get off the plane." Please: If there is nowhere for the rest of us to go, think about whether you really need to have that conversation. Nobody is going to die if you wait three minutes to make that call.

Is He Talking to Himself? Take business calls in an appropriate setting. Have you ever seen people talking on hands-free devices in a department store or sporting event? They can't possibly be coming across to their listeners as someone who is focused on business. Just because you can talk on the phone and shop at Wal-Mart does not mean it is the smart thing to do.

Call Waiting—Never. Just because you have call waiting does not mean you have to be controlled by it. When you put off the person that you are speaking with to answer another call, you are saying that the incoming call is more important. You can always call back when the first call is complete. Answer the second call only if you think it could be an emergency and even then explain the possibility.

No Need to Shout. When using a cell phone, speak normally. For whatever reason, many people talk at top volume when they are on a cell phone. Microphones are sensitive. The person you are calling can hear you and *we* don't need to.

Must You Talk Here? Please be considerate of others; those that are waiting on you and those in line behind you. Many times people talk on phones while in line, and then do not even address or acknowledge the employees whose assistance they need. What is really irritating is that they will then take their time getting out of the way, as if they are such important people that we all must wait for them to deal with their personal phone calls.

Your Competition May be Listening. Be aware that someone from a competing firm might be near enough to overhear your conversation about a client or prospect. They could possibly gather enough information to steal the opportunity from you.

Keep Your Private Affairs to Yourself. Discussing anything of a private nature on your cell phone in public is unwise on a number of counts. Unless you want to raise a lot of questions and eyebrows, wait until you have privacy to take calls from those who are likely to have unpleasant, upsetting, or incriminating information. Too much information given over a cell phone while others are within earshot could cost you dearly.

A friend shared this story, a woman waiting in line along with many other people began talking on her cell to a repairman who was going to her home—while she was not there. By the end of the call, she had given her address and directions on how to get there, and told him the location of the spare key! She even mentioned what time the repairman would be there and how long the job would take. Anyone could have reached the woman's house before the repairman got there and cleaned her out—or worse yet, watched for the repairman to leave and be waiting for her when she arrived back home. Be careful what you say on your cell phone in public. Not everyone is as honest as you and I.

Phones and Driving Should Not Mix. It seems like such a productive use of time, but driving and talking on the phone—even with hands-free devices—can be very distracting. Please consider our safety. If there are other cars on the road with you, don't be driving while dialing a number or talking on the cell phone. Pull off or wait until you get where you're going. Most people don't realize how distracted they are or how they react when talking on a cell phone. It's strange to me how people assume this rule is intended for *others*. Just remember to be mindful of who and what is going on around you when driving.

Taking Pictures Using Your Cell Phone. Use discretion and ask permission before taking pictures of anybody or the surroundings in a business setting with your cell phone. If in doubt about the appropriateness of taking a picture just don't do it. Some organizations are very guarded about their business and will not want pictures taken on their premises.

Texting. We've been using texting to communicate with friends and family for years, and it is now becoming acceptable to communicate with clients using texts. However, there is a difference. Be careful about typos. It may be OK to skip vowels or to not worry about spelling and punctuation with your friends, but with clients it sends a message that you are careless. If you use voice texting, check it before sending. It won't take that much more time to do it correctly, and will improve the impression you leave. It tells the client that he or she is worth the time to do it correctly. Always ask your clients if texts are acceptable or if they would prefer a phone call or e-mail. In order to preserve a lasting relationship, don't allow texting to completely replace phone calls or personal interactions. People will always do business with people.

Following these cell phone tips just might save your personal credibility, professional image, and maybe even your job.

Master Telephone Communication Skills. No matter where the lead comes from—referrals, networking, social media, or cold calling—you'll need to speak with that prospect on the telephone at some point. Master communication skills that enable you to speak with any prospect at any time and gain the response you want. This takes practice and focus, but once mastered it becomes second nature.

The ability to use the telephone effectively in business, especially for contacting potential new prospects and clients, creates value. Your business will grow more rapidly and you will be viewed as someone who has the ability to make things happen. Think of each phone call as a new beginning—a new slate. It's the opportunity to create something of value from nothing. Using the phone effectively is a valuable skill that can be cultivated with practice, so make it part of every day's Business Development activities. The more you do it—the easier it gets.

Connecting with people is fun, so just do it and keep moving forward. Probably nothing is going to happen if you don't *make* it happen, and picking up the phone is a good place to start.

"Even if you're on the right track, you are going to get run over if you just sit there!"

—Will Rogers

Key Concepts in this Chapter

1. The telephone can be a powerful Business Development tool when used properly.
2. It is important to schedule time to make phone calls and to develop a plan before making a call.
3. We discussed how to get around obstacles and how to effectively manage the conversation.
4. Leaving a voice message can be an opportunity to give a commercial.
5. Included is a list of rules for using the cell phone as a business tool.

8

THE INTRODUCTORY CLIENT MEETING

The Introductory Meeting. Congratulations! You've done all the right things and worked very hard to get to the right people at a prospective company that you have targeted. You've made phone calls, sent e-mails, and had a short introductory phone conversation with the right person. You've succeeded in setting up a meeting to learn more about the target firm and to speak with the decision-maker at that firm. Now, let's talk about that first meeting and how to make it work for you.

The purpose of the first meeting is to break the ice and to lay the groundwork for a relationship with this person and his or her company. Your goal is to form a trusting, long-lasting relationship so that the decision-maker thinks of you when he or she needs services such as those you can provide. Selling professional services is all about forming trusting relationships. Relationships are based on *face* time, but that face time must be constructive and of value to both you and the prospective client. Value can be assured by mastering the art of effective meeting conversations.

Technology has made it very easy for us to use tablets or other devices for one-on-one presentations. These are great in some situations and help to guide the conversation. Just make sure to use them as supportive tools and don't allow them to interfere with gaining an understanding of the client's needs.

Provide just enough information about you and your company to get the prospect interested, but the first meeting should be focused on getting him or her to do most of the talking. That's how you know this person is interested in developing the relationship. The more forthcoming the other person is with information, the more you can be sure this will be a mutually beneficial relationship.

Frame open-ended questions so that you get prospective clients talking, and then feed off what they say to gain further information. With good questions you get them doing most of the talking and you can focus on listening. If you listen, prospective clients will tell you what's important to them, how they feel, and how things work in their organizations. If you are doing all the talking, then you are not learning very much about the prospects, their problems, or how to take the relationship to the next level.

Planning the Conversation. As you prepare for this first meeting you should pull together key people in your organization and brainstorm. Literally sit down and plan what you will talk about and in what order. The questions you plan to ask will be based on who you are meeting with and what you want to learn. People who think they can just "wing it" are arrogant and fooling themselves. While it's true that you have no way of knowing what the prospect's answers will be, you can plan your questions and the general direction of the conversation. This way you will come across as a professional, showing respect and value for everyone's time.

Do your research by visiting the company's website and each individual's LinkedIn page. Have an idea of what the issues might be, but plan to be flexible and follow the path laid out as the conversation unfolds. When you do research and plan, you prove to prospects that you cared enough to be prepared.

As you are planning, think through the possible outcomes of the meeting so that you can follow whatever direction the conversation goes, but have a clear goal in mind of what you want to achieve. Contrary to what some may think, constructive client conversations don't just happen. Thinking ahead provides clarity for you and guides the information-gathering process. Pre planning a meeting can be very powerful in the Business Development process.

First, ask yourself a few questions:

1. Is this a discovery meeting where we will just get acquainted and see where it goes?
2. Is there a specific project we are targeting? What do we need to know about it?
3. Is this a current client that has voiced a concern and to whom I might offer new services?
4. Am I asking for introductions to other departments?
5. Is there a competitor already in place? Do we need to show how we can do a better job?
6. What will be the next step? How can I position for that meeting?
7. What actions do I need to take before the next call?
8. What are my strengths and weaknesses going into this meeting?

By gathering all this information, you will feel more confident and ready for your meeting. Thinking and planning ahead leaves your mind free to listen to the client as he or she speaks, which will give you the freedom to be flexible.

Keep in mind that Business Development for professional services is a journey—not an event. While it might look simple on paper, and somewhat easy to explain, the sales process for professional services is more a series of loops.

For example, the first step, and the purpose of this first meeting, is the identification of a problem or issue. It is not a single step, but a gradual evolution of knowledge gathered a piece at a time. To jump to a conclusion after obtaining a single piece of the problem is to have an incomplete picture. You need to be the tour guide and ask the right questions that allow both you and the prospect to clearly define the problem.

Once the problem is clear, then your job is to gather additional information about it—that's the next loop. With each new piece of information, perception and understanding changes, moving backward and forward. Your job at this point is to move the discovery process along with the prospect as understanding develops.

The next loop is where the various options become apparent. As you begin to evaluate different options, loops may blur as the different options are considered. New knowledge may surface. It's best not to try to control the agenda too strictly, in order to let the series of loops interconnect where they should. By allowing flexibility, you entrench yourself as a trusted partner. The loops will continue to form even after your meeting or as the project ends. There will be follow-up that uncovers new opportunities, and the process starts again.

Create an Agenda. Seasoned people may not feel that making a meeting plan is necessary, but it really does not take that much time, and it creates a more focused meeting structure that produces better results. Creating an agenda helps everyone understand the meeting's focus. Think about such things as: Why did this person agree to see you in the first place? What is the person trying to do with the business? What are the company's goals? What challenge is the company likely to be facing? From there you will determine what open-ended questions to ask to gain the information you need so that you can help this client.

Set the Tone of the Relationship. Speak and appear professional at all times, and dress one step above how the client will be dressed. Keep in mind that the client is going to pay your firm a great deal of money. Would you be comfortable going to a doctor who dressed as if he or she did not care about appearance? Appearance creates a perception, and in the professional services world, perception is everything. Be professional, but don't try to create a business persona and adopt a "sales" tone. Just be yourself.

Never lie or stretch the truth; it's not worth it. You have your own reputation and your company's credibility to be concerned about. Always treat a prospect with respect, just as you would want to be treated—politely and respectfully. This does not mean it is necessary to be a brownnoser. Becoming too friendly too soon can create suspicion and distrust, so give the prospect plenty of time to get to know you.

This meeting is focused on the client. Don't talk about how busy you are, or else you may create the perception that you don't have time to give the client's project your full attention. However, you don't want the other person to think you have nothing to do, either, because then he or she might think you are not very good at what you do. The best answer to a question on the topic is: "Business is great, but we are always looking for new challenges." Avoid politics, religion, or any other sensitive subject.

Arrive about ten minutes early to allow time to check in and get through security if required. Spend a couple of minutes getting yourself calmed down and ready to visit with your prospective new client. Enjoy the opportunity to make a new friend.

The conversation is where the relationship and the rapport will begin. The introductory conversation will generally follow three phases: the personal connection, the discovery or fishing phase, and the closing phase. Each phase requires a different set of questions to gather the information you need.

Personal Chemistry. Relax and be yourself. If others are with you, introduce them and explain their roles. When other people attend from the other firm, understand the responsibilities of each so that your remarks to them can be tailored accordingly.

Take a few minutes as you arrive to remind your prospect of any connection you might have—a mutual friend or networking organization—and then exchange a few bits of get-acquainted information such as family, sports, or news items. You might glance around the person's office for topics that will be of interest to him or her.

Reconfirm the time that the prospect has available for this meeting. It would not be good to believe you have an hour when the other person is thinking only thirty minutes. If your prospect indicates that an emergency has come up and the meeting will need to be cut short, it would be best to use this short time to get acquainted, but get a commitment for another time. You don't want to hurry through this most important first meeting.

Take Your Time. Don't be in rush, but don't waste time, either. If you jump into the business side of the conversation too quickly, it creates a tense atmosphere. Follow the other person's lead and gauge when to start talking business and how much small talk is enough—usually about five or ten minutes is enough. Timing is everything. The prospect expects this to be a business meeting. However, if you start business talk too early, it comes across as abruptness. If you take too long to get to the point, the client may begin to wonder, "Are we ever going to get going here? I have other things to do."

Value the client's time; he or she may be billable, too. It may be costing this person money when they stop to talk with you. Other people's time is valuable and it is important to recognize that. Let people know that you realize their time is valuable and that you appreciate it. You might say something like this: "I know your time is valuable, too, so I will be direct." By using the word "too," you help him or her realize that *your* time is also valuable.

Make the Connection. Making a solid connection with another person can be as simple as combining the right balance of talking and questioning. It's usually better if the other person does most of the talking, but you need to guide the conversation through effective questioning. If you ask too many questions too quickly, it can come across as interrogation. On the other hand, if you talk too much, the other person will find you boring and tune out. Somewhere in the middle is where you want to be. Make sure you are actively listening and that the other person is talking about 70 percent of the time. Building real rapport will not be possible unless the prospect feels that you are tuned in and care about what he or she has to say.

Be willing to listen to what the prospect values and show interest in his or her interests in order to build trust. Most people are self-focused. It's not wrong; it's just the way it is. Recognizing and capitalizing on that tendency can actually work in your favor at this first meeting. It can help you to gather information about the individual in order to understand how you can relate in an effective way.

In this first meeting, the prospect will instinctively decide if there is a likability factor or if a personal chemistry is established. Most of the buying decision—about 80 percent—will be based on how the prospect feels about you. Your personal interactions are what build a positive connection.

Suggested open-ended questions for your first meeting:

- "How familiar are you with our company?" (This question tells you if you need to further explain your company offerings. Probably not. You gave this person a brief overview when setting up this meeting, and chances are he or she has visited your website so there is no need to go into details again. If you've been asked to come in and present your company capabilities, then the meeting will require a different format than you would use for the first meeting. This meeting is about the prospect and learning all you can about the prospect's situation.)
- "Tell me about your responsibilities."
- "On the website I noticed that your CEO values _____. What does that mean for you? How does that impact your job?"
- "What type of project does your group manage?"
- "How has the (a current issue such as the economy, regulatory driver, or political event) affected your operations?"

Discovery Period. Once rapport has been established, you will begin the discovery period of uncovering the prospect's issues and concerns. Your goal is to find a specific problem or project for which you can provide a solution. The tendency is to think about what clients need in relation to the services you have to offer, but at this point you are just trying to make a connection and to uncover the true needs. Many of the true needs may be unspoken. You should not be selling during this first meeting—you are simply gathering information.

This is a crucial step in the Business Development process. When you uncover his or her issues and concerns, you have grounds for offering your service solutions in a way that will benefit the client. Unless you can uncover the true issues, you will always be working in the dark. Get a handle on the real issues and concerns as early as possible, and you have information that will keep you well ahead of the competition with this prospective client. If you have the same information that is available to every other firm, then you will always be struggling to differentiate your firm.

Using your own style and words, ask three to five of the right open-ended questions to direct the conversation. Open-ended questions begin with *what*, *how*, and *why*. Asking such questions will help uncover any needs, opinions, values, priorities, and sensitivities. Don't fire the questions one after the other; ask your question and then *stop talking* while the other person answers. Never interrupt, and don't ask another question until you are sure the other person has told you everything he or she wants to say.

By asking the right questions you can guide the conversation that helps the prospect to recall information that will be useful. If the prospect wanders off into another area that is obviously not going to provide useful information, gently guide him or her back by asking another relevant question, or repeat the same one in a different way.

Some information may be subtle, so ask for clarification on that particular piece of information. Listen closely, and then in a natural way probe and clarify for a deeper understanding: "Can you tell me more about that?" "What do you mean?" By probing further, you encourage the client to provide you with more information about the situation or the project. Some things may surface that he or she has not thought of previously. Make sure the prospect sees the benefit of providing you with the information you are requesting.

Using the client's language and industry terminology, choose from some of these as general ideas for your questions:

- What are some of the issues and concerns you will be facing this year?

- What are you doing about _____? (When you ask this question, the prospect understands that your company can do that kind of work.)
- Can you give me some background on your situation? How did it start? How long has it been going on? What will happen if this does not get resolved?
- What is your personal interest? (Find out where it hurts personally.)
- What would you like to see happen?
- What did you like about your previous consultant?
- What went well on your previous project? (By asking this type of question, you'll learn what the prospect values and what he or she does not like.)
- When does the project need to be completed?
- What is the budget range?
- Ask about project parameters that can be of value—size, number of people, etc.

Closing. Keep an eye on the time. It's your job to make the most of this valuable time you have asked for—both the prospect's time and yours. By directing the conversation with questions, you help the other person focus and use the time efficiently. When you reach the end of the time that was requested when the appointment was made, the professional thing to do is to begin to close. If the prospect obviously wants to continue, then let him or her be the guide on when to end the meeting.

Suggestions for closing questions:

- "What would you suggest as our next step?"
- "Where do we go from here?"
- "How often should we follow up with you?"
- "Would you like a proposal on this project?"
- "What will be the decision-making process?"

- "Are you considering other firms?"
- "Who will the decision-makers be?"
- "When will the decision be made?"
- "Where do we go from here?"
- "When would you suggest we follow up with you again?"
- "Are there others in the company that we should know?"

Moving this relationship to the next level may be as simple as asking for an introduction to others in the organization that this person would suggest that you meet. They could be part of the selection committee, or a potential decision-maker. Prepare for multiple meetings to ensure forward movement. Think through the logical outcomes of each of those meetings.

The key takeaways from your first meetings are to talk less and listen more. By talking less and asking the right questions, you will quickly establish rapport and the beginnings of a long-term successful relationship with a prospective client that you have chosen.

Plan and schedule follow-up. Ask when and how to follow up. Confirm action items and set a date for the next step. Thank your contact and the others for their time, and show appreciation for the value of the information they shared.

Listening. How you listen is just as important as the questions you ask. Be truly interested. Hear what the other person is saying, and be aware of the message of your body language.

- o Lean forward and focus on the speaker.
- o Take notes (it's your way of showing the information is important to you).
- o Nod occasionally to acknowledge the significance of the information.

    o   Smile and use the appropriate facial expressions to show empathy for what is said.

Make it a point to observe what is *not* being said. Observe the other person's level of eye contact and body language. Visible changes in tension and emotions can tell you a lot about the emotional level of the issue.

How do you balance talking enough to educate and asking the right questions to gather the information you need? If you are doing most of the talking, then you can be sure you are not orchestrating the right balance. Many people fall into the trap of talking too much because they believe they should show the client their expertise. They may get nervous and start talking about their company too much, or asking too many questions without waiting for the client to share. Slow down.

When you are working too hard to show your expertise, you are missing a lot of information. Buyers of professional services want to buy more than just your expertise and solutions—they want a relationship with a trusted advisor.

If you are doing all the talking, you will fail to pick up on signals that tell you what you need to know. You may also miss out on an opportunity to provide a solution to a bigger problem than what you thought was the issue at the beginning of the conversation. Let the other person talk, and you will learn so much more. Also, when you truly listen, show interest and ask insightful questions; you demonstrate what it will be like to work with you.

Help your client to tell his or her story. Everyone loves to talk about themselves and to tell their story. If not given the opportunity to do so, your client will feel ignored, overwhelmed, and unheard. Focus on how you can help, rather than on what you want to say. The best conversations you will have are those when you are focused on helping the client succeed. Ask open-ended questions and then shut up and listen. The more you listen, the easier it will be to find the perfect solution and to build that very important trust.

Moving to the Sales Phase. In future meetings you will want to move into a more of a sales approach focused on particular projects. Professional services are seldom "sold." It works best to present the business case for your offered solution and allow clients to sell themselves. Help clients see the gap or difference between where they are currently and where they want to be.

While the emotional impact on the prospect is of great importance, you need to be able to make the business case for him or her to engage you and your services. If you are not able to make a business case, you will be at a disadvantage throughout the relationship. Clarify the value and impact of working with you, because prospects cannot always know the true value at the beginning. Don't assume that the other person understands; make it very clear for him or her.

Methods to clarify the impact include:

1. *Financial.* Compare the cost savings or the impact of doing nothing versus the cost of having it not done properly the first time. Provide examples such as: "We saved the XYZ Company $2 million by doing this for them." "It cost ZYX Company $1 million for us to correct the job that was done poorly by another firm."
2. *Emotions.* Speak to the person; explain the peace of mind, promotion, or job security this decision can bring. While you must be able to show the financial impact, ultimately people buy with their emotions—it's how they justify it in their heads and hearts.

3. *Impact vs. the alternative.* Show the impact of not working with you, or of working with an alternative company. Never speak negatively about the competition; just be able to discuss how your service is superior by giving examples of previous projects.

4. *Contribution to ROI.* Know the alternatives and be able to show how the prospect can succeed by working with you versus the competition.

5. *Consequences of not moving forward.* The prospect may be able see the value of working with you, but not the negative impacts if he or she does not move forward. By asking the prospect what will happen if he or she does not move forward, you are probing for the consequences of inaction and moving your company to a higher position.

6. *Examples.* Build credibility with discussions of similar impacts that you've experienced yourself, and show how you may have dealt with a similar situation and decision.

7. *Make it Tangible.* A professional service by nature is an intangible item. If you can paint a picture or tell a story, it helps the client identify with the tangible rather than having it feel so abstract. Be able to depict what is going to change when your service is engaged. Show a tangible value articulated in dollars, efficiencies, or in a resolution to a problem.

Because you are offering a service that is complex and intangible, prospects often have a hard time knowing exactly what they are buying and what the value will be. You will need to paint the picture of the new reality and its value, and how it is best for the customer based on your knowledge of their issues and concerns. Start the process by creating a situation that encourages creative thinking. Ask insightful questions and then be silent, giving the prospect time to envision the future. Silence on your part also shows that you are actively listening.

In the future, when it is time to present your proposal, use those same pictures, graphs, and tables to tell the story of how you will address the issues and concerns that were uncovered in the first meeting. If a picture is worth a thousand words, then you should use lots of pictures and graphs. The goal is to paint a compelling picture of your client's new reality of a successful project.

The solution stage is where you craft an idea and articulate how you can help. At this stage, stay focused on just what the prospect needs and resists the urge to offer everything. The prospect won't hear it anyway, if he or she doesn't need it. When the relationship is new, you may want to break the solution into smaller phases or projects rather than jumping in too big at the start. As you move to subsequent phases, trust builds and the relationship is more solid and supportive.

After the Meeting. Upon completion of your visit, send a thank-you note for the person's time and include any information you promised to send. It's most impressive when the note is handwritten, because it is so rare these days to receive a "real" piece of mail.

Follow Up. Schedule your next action or follow-up with this contact. Continue to follow up for as long as it takes to either get an opportunity, or to determine that no opportunity exists. If there is not an opportunity, remove such contacts from your target list so that you keep it clean and focused on the right targets. That's not to say you will forget about them; it's just that there are only so many hours in the day and you need to focus your time where it is most beneficial.

Enter notes and other information into a contact management system. Do it as soon as possible, because you will not recall the fine details of the conversation a month from now. That one tidbit of information might mean the difference between winning the work or not. Sometimes pieces of information about a prospect and a potential opportunity can be more valuable next year than it is today.

Enter any identified project into a tracking system. It is important that leads not fall through the cracks, so they need to go into some sort of lead-tracking system. Without the proper follow-up, the value of all the information you've worked so hard to gather will be lost.

Develop a Capture Plan

When an opportunity is identified, it will save you time later, and make your efforts more focused, if you will develop a capture plan for that prospect as soon as possible. This is a document that lists all the key players, a description of the potential projects, the time frame involved, your thoughts on how to approach it, the team members you want to involve, and any facts that will help win the job. The document outlines what the Business Development process looks like for the prospect.

The capture plan is a document that can be accessed by other team members and can bring them up to speed quickly—all the information about a particular target is in one place. This is where you will list client issues and concerns and any other pieces of information that will be necessary to use in capturing this opportunity. The capture plan can be used to gather all information and to outline and schedule follow-up activities. It can be used to make assignments to other team members that may help pursue this opportunity. It gives them all the information needed in one document. See a suggested capture plan form at the end of the chapter.

Be Persistent. Intelligent persistence is the key to successful Business Development. Keep moving forward—in my experience 80 percent of all sales are made after the ninth contact. Most people, your competitors, are probably going to give up after the second contact. This is why it is important to be persistent about making follow-up contacts.

Continue to make many contacts with this person. What counts as a contact? Anything that keeps you top of mind; phone calls, voice mail, meeting at a networking event, mailings, articles, face-to-face meetings, and other forms of follow-up. Everyone has different methods, but be sure to find ways to keep up with this prospect especially if there is a known project coming out, until at least nine contacts have been made.

Don't Be a Pest. Where is the balance between becoming a pest and being persistent with follow-up? A lot has to do with knowing what will be of value to the prospective client and how often he or she *said* you should follow up. Anything that is of value to the prospective client is good follow-up material. You will be perceived as a pest only if you are bringing no value, and the prospect feels that you are only interested in getting something from him or her. Ask how often you should follow up, and take his or her lead on how often to call. The prospect will tell you, if you ask politely and make it clear that you don't want to be a bother but want to be of service and support.

Stay in Touch. Even if people know you personally, and you feel that you have established an excellent rapport, they may not always think of you or remember the services that you can provide to them—which is why you must continue to tell them as often as possible. People are busy just like we are, and their days are filled with many distractions. Here are some interesting facts about conversations.

- The average person forgets half of what you say to him or her by the end of the first day.
- The average person will forget 90 percent by the end of the first week and probably 100 percent by the next month.
- Within six months the person may not even remember meeting you, unless you bring something of value that makes it worthwhile for him or her to remember.

Use notes you made during your visit to the person's office to help with future interactions. You can ask about children or grandchildren, favorite sports teams, news events, or anything of personal interest.

Send your contact web or news articles—not only about business-related topics, but also about personal hobbies or subjects that you know he or she will be interested in learning. Maybe you learned this from your first visit, from things you observed in the person's office or LinkedIn page, or from talking to other people. Is the client a white-water rafting enthusiast, golfer, or an antique car buff? You might think about the person's position in the firm and things that would be of interest to him or her because of that. Add follow-up ideas to your schedule.

Visuals. Using visuals in your conversation will help people remember you and your conversation. Most of the new people that you meet with will need to hear about your company capabilities and the benefit you bring several times before it sticks. It's similar to commercial advertisements—we only pay attention to the new car advertisements when we are interested in buying a new car. Potential clients will most likely not remember all of the services that your company can provide unless they need that particular service at the time. So stay in touch, make a visual impact, and keep saying it!

Be Concise. In your communications, be concise and direct; don't assume that the other person understands what you mean. Keep in mind that what you actually say to someone is not as important as what he or she *hears* you say. It's good to ask for feedback periodically to be sure that your message is coming across as you intended. This is another reason that it's best to meet with prospects and to talk face-to-face. People are more likely to understand and remember what you tell them when you have had a sit-down meaningful conversation.

Different Personality Types. You will be dealing with many different personality types and it helps to have an understanding of how best to relate to them.

Introverts tend to give short concise responses to your questions. You have to probe for additional information by using phrases such as, "How does that work for you?" or "I would like to know more about that." Ask probing questions to gain a deeper understanding and to get the person thinking past short replies. Another thing about introverts is that they will usually take time to analyze and mentally craft their reply before speaking. You may have to stop and wait a couple of minutes before they speak. Control the urge to help by finishing their sentences. Don't do it—just be patient and relate at their pace.

The opposite end of that spectrum will be the person that does not know when to stop talking. A good way to manage the conversation is to say something like, "I know you are busy and don't want to take up too much of your time." Then ask your next question.

Some people like to feel in control, and others may be timid. Not everybody will be the same, so be prepared to find a way to relate to people of each personality type on their own terms.

What if...? There are some common situations that seem to happen frequently when conversing with clients and prospects.

What if the prospect won't stop talking? In the first conversations, this can be good for you. Listening builds trust, and by listening with interest you help the other person to feel more relaxed with you. However, when the information is no longer useful you may have to redirect the conversation. You can say, "I see what you are saying and it reminds me of something I would like to share with you." Some people just don't see when it's time to stop talking.

What if the prospect asks a negative question? For example, he or she might ask negative questions such as, "Why are your rates so high?" Just turn the question into a positive by rephrasing it, "You asked about our rates," and then proceed to explain what is involved in your pricing structure.

What if the prospect unexpectedly brings multiple decision-makers to your meeting? The more people involved the better for you, if handled properly. Understand how they fit into the organization. Address everyone and make eye contact, no matter their position. Be courteous and show your professionalism.

What if the prospect brings up the competition? Avoid criticism of the competition. Find something good to say and then show how your company can be a better choice. For example, "XYZ has been around for a long time; however, from what you have told me, I believe our company can better meet your needs for this project." Then you can repeat the points that prove that statement.

Know Who Can Help You Make the Sale. A key is to understand the impact that each individual has on the decision to choose your company for the work. Gauge each person's level of influence by watching for critical clues. These are some of the clues that tell you who can help you the most in order to affect the outcome of the solution you wish to provide:

- An individual's organizational impact to a particular department. When a project will involve a particular department, those involved with that department would likely have a higher degree of influence.
- A person's position in the company and experience level will determine the amount of influence he or she will have on the decision. Somebody with ten or more years at the company will probably

have more say, and be more respected for what they have to say, than somebody who is new to the company.

- People who will be directly impacted are more likely to have a say in the decision.
- When a person stands to gain as part of a personal priority, he or she is likely to have a stronger say in the decision. The person feels a personal stake in the outcome.
- Internal politics can carry significant weight. Align yourself with the person who has the most internal advocates.

Additional Tips. Communication during a first meeting, and subsequent meetings, can sometimes be tricky, but can be very rewarding when managed properly. Your conversation will be the basis for a continuing relationship.

- Practice will make it much easier to know what to say and do at the right time during conversations.
- If the other person asks you a question, be sure you understand *why* this person is asking before you begin to answer.
- Never interrupt. Wait until the speaker completes his or her thought—the information that you did not plan for may be the most valuable information you will gather! Make a note to come back to a point you want to talk about, but let the other person finish.
- When the other person talks about his or her issues and concerns, then it is very likely that he or she wants them to go away.
- Each issue that surfaces will provide you with the opportunity to make an impact on this person's business.
- Uncovering and discussing a problem will many times lead to other issues that the prospect may not have thought of in the beginning. Proper questioning helps to uncover them.

- Be listening for the other person's aspirations and dreams because you can help with those, too. Maybe the thing that is keeping this individual up at night is not related to problems or issues, but the excitement that comes from growth and possibilities.
- Goals and aspirations are future-minded topics for conversations and may drive the relationship to a higher level more quickly. When you determine that the other person's thoughts are focused on the future, your goal is to help him or her see how you can be a part of achieving those dreams.

Face-to-face meetings are important to building a professional services business. Different service type firms will have different methods of meeting each step of the process. The purpose is to make sure you work through all the steps in order to create a strong relationship. The stronger the relationship, the more difficult it will be for the competition to steal your client.

Prospective Client Capture Plan

	SECTOR	Date Completed

☐	Company/ Organization:
	    Contact:
	      Title:
	      Address:
	      Phones:
	      E-mail:	

☐	Our manager for this client (include others that may be involved):	

☐	Conduct Research (learn as much as possible about prospect; check website, news items)
	   • Other office locations
	   • Other people we need to meet
	   • Services they need
	   • News items
	   • Potential opportunities	

☐	Conduct internal research (*gather knowledge of who has contacts or previous experience at this company*)	

☐	First meeting plan
	   • Introduce yourself and the company; direct them to our website
	   • Preplan open-ended questions
	   • Offer to conduct a Lunch & Learn (try to set a date as soon as they seem interested)
	   • Send any additional information based on your conversation
	   • Set future meeting	

☐	Add to newsletter mailing list	
☐	Conduct a general services presentation	
☐	Send handwritten "thank you for your time" note to each person attending	

☐	Identify project opportunities and add to tracking sheet
	   • Time frame
	   • Potential revenue	

☐	Send more detailed SOQ or additional follow-up information	
☐	Schedule next steps and follow-up	
☐	Schedule lunch meetings with key individuals (list them and the scheduled dates)	

☐	EXISTING client—we already know the key people and their needs:
	   o Schedule regular contacts
	   o Conduct satisfaction interviews
	   o Offer technical Lunch & Learn (can be on a subject of interest to them; use projects as example case studies)	

☐	Who else do we need to know in the organization (would contact be willing to make introductions)	
☐	Determine potential new work opportunities	
☐	Periodically send articles or information that may be of interest	
☐	Schedule to meet on a regular basis—quarterly, monthly, etc. "Drop in" for a visit if the company allows it. Walk around and meet others while in the building.	
☐	NETWORKING: Regularly attend networking events and conferences that this client will attend. List potential events and dates.	
☐	Invite them to a social event that fits their interest: golf, fishing…	
	ACTION ITEMS and Additional Notes:	

Key Concepts in this Chapter

1. The introductory meeting can be stressful unless you are clear on what you are trying to accomplish.
2. The first meeting is important because it will lay the groundwork for a long-term relationship with the client.
3. Develop a plan for client meetings and involve others that can contribute.
4. Ask the right open-ended questions to uncover how your firm can be of service. Included are suggestions for effective open-ended questions.
5. Listening can be just as important as talking.
6. Develop a Client Capture Plan (example above) using the information that outlines each step in the process of turning this prospect into a long-term client.

9

BUILDING CLIENT LOYALTY THROUGH COMMUNICATION

Interpersonal communication is the key to success in everything we do—at work or in our personal lives. Communication skills are required to keep clients happy and to be able to work with difficult coworkers. In our personal lives, communication skills can make the difference between having a happy and peaceful life and one that is filled with stress.

Client Maintenance. Everyone in the firm is involved with client maintenance using various communication tools. Client maintenance includes more than just the marketing and Business Development departments; it includes every employee in the firm. More than one client has been lost because they felt they were not a priority. These clients were made to feel this way due to miscommunication, or worse—no communication.

A client may be very pleased with the project work but uncomfortable with the accounting department's attention to details for invoicing, rudeness of the person that answers the phone, or a lack of responsiveness from project managers. Any of these will leave a client unsure of your company's level of quality and capabilities.

Foundation for Trust. People who share information about their needs and concerns have a better foundation for trust. Taking an extra interest in existing clients and their industries is part of the equation for loyal clients. This interest cannot be superficial and should never be forced. Doing good work is important and may be what gets you in the door, but it is not the total equation. The client must feel trust for the company that is providing services. Expecting the client to hand you the next project just because the previous one went well is not likely to happen without forming a strong and trusting relationship between the two firms. Gaining credibility and earning respect and endorsement of the client is an ongoing process and can only be done through effective communication.

Measure Client Satisfaction. One of the best ways to find out how a client feels about your company's level of service, and to measure the client's expectations, is to ask the client! It can be difficult, but it is best to be forthright in communication in order to gain the information needed. Ask the right questions and then probe for additional details. Some firms want to avoid talking with their clients about problem areas for fear that they will hear something they do not want to hear—but that's when it's needed the most! You should want the client to tell *you* rather than someone else.

Communication is important because you want to learn about any silent dissatisfaction as early as possible. You want to know before it becomes part of the grapevine and before the problem magnifies itself. When something goes wrong on a project, you can't afford to fool yourself into thinking that it is an isolated incident and not a big deal. Whether we like it or not, people talk to each other. You want to be able to control what they talk about!

In order for client maintenance to have a positive effect, it must be a part of the overall Business Development efforts of your company. Client

176

maintenance has more to do with accelerating, enhancing, and improving ongoing relationships than any other Business Development effort. Ideally these relationships will provide additional work opportunities and improve revenue from existing clients, as well as improve your credibility in the industry. The more you communicate directly with the client, the better your competitive advantage.

It's important to have a solid knowledge of your clients' needs and true issues behind their needs and concerns. Having this solid knowledge puts you well ahead of the competition and builds customer loyalty. If there are negative comments, respond to them before they grow out of proportion. It also provides an opportunity to discuss new projects or needs that the client may have in the future, and to talk about trends in the market.

Why Clients Leave. Why do professional services firms lose clients? Generally clients leave for one (or more) of the following reasons:

1. The client no longer has a need.
2. The client has had a bad experience.
3. Lack of communication tells clients that you take his or her business for granted or are not interested anymore.
4. The client feels that you no longer view his or her project as a priority.
5. Too many misunderstandings due to poor communication leave the client wondering if you know what you are doing.
6. The client believes that inertia has taken place and wants fresh ideas from new people.
7. The client believes that another person or firm can better understand his or her needs.

The majority of these reasons can be influenced by developing a stronger relationship with the client from the very beginning through better communication. People will often forget what you said to them, but they never forget how you made them feel. Make sure the people you interact with feel important and understood.

There are many ways to understand and develop more lasting relationships through better communications, with existing or previous clients:

1. One of the best ways to build relationships is continuous on-the-job communication and should be cultivated on a daily basis. Other more formal methods of client communication would be to call the client for no reason except to touch base and to ask how things are going. Call with updates on the client's project or a similar project that he or she might be interested in knowing about.

2. Anonymous surveys, via mail or electronic format, are very inexpensive. Clients can give feedback without having to face anybody personally. This should be done for all clients, especially at the close of a project. A disadvantage with anonymous surveys is a low response rate and the inability to obtain details and an immediate understanding of the client's thinking. There is also a limited ability to assess the potential for future work. Not having a verbal exchange diminishes the effectiveness of such information.

3. A telephone survey or conversation provides a certain protective wall for the client. Phone surveys can be very effective, especially if done by someone other than the project manager; the client feels freer to give a more unbiased response. It's best to let the client know ahead of time the type of questions that will be asked so that he or she will have time to think about a response. More meaningful information can be gathered this way than through anonymous surveys, because you can build upon and probe for additional information as issues are brought up.

4. The personal face-to-face interview is the most effective. While it may be cost prohibitive to talk with all clients using personal interviews, it should be done with at least the top 20 percent of revenue-producing

clients—both existing and previous. Studies have proven that meeting face-to-face gives far better results than any other method and can greatly improve the learning curve for any company process improvements. In professional service firms, people are serving other people and communication is just more effective when conducted face-to-face. You can only be sure that a client's expectations are being met by interacting with them one-on-one and asking them. The approach may vary, depending on the level of relationship and the desired objectives for the information gathered.

Understand the Client. It is important to understand why your clients value their relationship with your company. Realizing that each client is an individual and their companies are different, it is important to understand their needs and concerns. Much of the communication used to gain the knowledge necessary for client maintenance should take place directly with the client and hopefully while on the project. It is also important to realize that strong relationships take time and must be based on mutual goals. You can never assume that you know what clients want. You must ask them.

Share knowledge about the clients with each other internally, especially if there are negative issues that continue to be repeated—you need to know what to do in order to avoid similar situations in the future. The development of a communication method used to share and store the important information that has been gained can increase your understanding of that particular client as well as interactions with other clients in the future.

Always be consistent in how you relate to clients—same personality, same type of dress and behavior—because sending the same signals helps to build trust. Be natural as if talking to a friend, but be mindful of maintaining a professional image.

Resolving Conflict Without Losing the Client. When you find yourself in a conflict situation with an existing client, it's important to tactfully bring the issue to the surface by talking about it. You've worked very hard to gain this client's account and you don't want to lose it as a result of misunderstanding.

Use active listening skills to echo back what the person is saying, asking for clarity on issues that might be misunderstood. Reflect back the person's feelings and body language by subtly mirroring his or her demeanor and style. It also helps to summarize what you understood, for clarity. Always take notes so that when the emotions calm down you can refer to the facts. Active listening puts the person at ease and validates what he or she is saying. When you listen sympathetically, it uncovers the hidden aspects of the situation—which may turn out to be different from the words being said. Listen for unspoken fears and concerns in order to connect with the true meanings behind the words.

Controversial Issues. When dealing with controversial issues, keep in mind that how something is phrased and how information is presented can be more meaningful than what is actually being said. Never insult another person's intelligence or appear to be confrontational. Try something like this:

- May I offer an idea?
- Would you be open to an alternative idea?
- There are a number of ways to approach this—what do you think about...?
- Would it be OK if I suggested another idea?
- May I offer a suggestion?
- In order to accomplish what you want, do you think it would be better to do it this way?

By presenting what you want to say in the form of a question, you are able to get your point across while allowing the client to save face. It may also allow you to salvage broken or strained relationships.

Following discussion of any issues or concerns, tell the client what you intend to do about the situation. Most times there are small painless adjustments that can be made to rectify the situation, and in doing so you've gone a long way toward gaining credibility and the client's respect.

In order for clients to feel that they are partners in the success of their projects, make an effort to communicate by listening more than you talk—by asking the right questions. When conducting a review or a satisfaction interview with a client, the client should be doing most of the talking. You want to plan ahead so that you can ask the right questions that will guide the conversation in the direction you want it to go. To avoid misunderstandings with new or existing clients, strive to gain complete clarity at the beginning of and during the project.

Try some of these open-ended questions for project-related discussion with each other at your own company or with the client:

- What are you trying to accomplish?
- How does this get done currently? Who does it?
- What are the limitations to the current approach?
- What is new about our approach? How does it bring value?
- Why do we think we can be successful at this time?
- If we succeed, what difference will it make?
- How long do we think it will take? What are our milestones?
- What it is the expected budget? How much will it cost?

Stick with the standard approach of asking: *What? Why? When? Where? How? How Much?* ...and always the most important question to be answered: *So What?*

Responding to Criticism. When you are in the business of serving other humans, it will happen. You will receive criticism and there will be conflicts. Whether it's true or not really doesn't matter—it's how you handle it that will make the difference between maintaining a loyal client and creating an enemy. You must remain professional while defusing the situation and seeking a solution.

When criticism is received, the first instinct is to become defensive. The situation becomes emotionally charged. You may produce an excuse, become angry, or dismiss the comment as unfounded or invalid. No matter how you feel about it, you must deal with the comment in a positive way. The criticism may render you momentarily speechless—you're shocked. The next instinct is to fight back. Neither reaction is very productive.

Respond in a positive and structured way by following four basic steps:

1. **Paraphrase.** This first step can be very powerful. Not only does it defuse a potentially charged atmosphere, it requires very little thought. Just repeat back what you heard in your own words. Your response should begin with, "It sounds like..." or "I can see that ..." You are not saying that you agree, and you're not apologizing or taking blame. You are simply lowering the other person's defenses by understanding and hearing what he or she has to say. It's a sign of respect. Everybody has a right to their opinion. They sometimes don't deliver the message in a tactful way.

2. **Listen.** This step is most difficult in a charged situation. Once you've paraphrased, stop talking. Give the other person back the floor and listen to what he or she has to say. We all share a universal urge to blurt out comments to

defend ourselves, but this is not the time if you want to salvage this client. Remind yourself it's not really about you, even if he or she uses the "you" word. By allowing the other person the floor and listening, you gather information that will help you understand what the underlying true issue is in the situation. It might be different than what was initially stated.

3. **Acknowledge**. Next, acknowledge the criticism, thus validating the other person's feelings. For example, when somebody says that this project is a disaster because of you, your acknowledgment might be something like: "I can understand your feelings. This project has not gone as we planned and has been a disappointment to all of us. Allow me to walk you through the changes we will be putting in place." Acknowledgment and respect are powerful because they enable the other person to feel understood and respected. You can then move on to put the conversation on safer ground that helps you both to move toward a joint solution.

4. **Negotiate**. If you agree, then you simply move to a joint solution, but what if you don't agree? The natural instinct is to frame a response in negative terms as to what can't be done. Turn it around to a more positive can-do response: "I plan to investigate the situation and let you know when I have a solution to the situation" or "I would like to hear what you believe to be the answer to this issue." Include the other person in the resolution to the problem.

This method of managing a charged situation is simple, logical, and free of emotion. Once you become accustomed to using this simple four-step process, you will be amazed at how much easier it becomes to manage criticism directed at you.

Client Satisfaction Interviews

Good client communication requires frequent contact in order to avoid issues before they turn into problems. Conducting a client satisfaction survey periodically with existing clients will help to reveal unvoiced concerns before they grow. Good times to conduct a client interview or review may be at the beginning of a project, during the project depending on how long it lasts, or at least annually. Conducting reviews with top revenue producers will track existing client perceptions. Interviews also provide a valid reason to contact previous clients. Asking for information about previous performance can bring them back as existing clients.

Asking for feedback about your service and how they feel about the company is important for several reasons:

1. It creates customer confidence in your desire to continuously improve your service.
2. The client will be impressed that you care about his or her opinion. He or she feels a sense of appreciation, partnership, value, and importance.
3. It opens the door to discuss future work and helps to determine the client's precise requirements. At the same time, the client explains how you can improve and better meet his or her expectations, thus giving you actionable items that drive the continuous improvement for your company.
4. The information obtained tells you what you are doing right and gives you a benchmark.
5. Primarily it is the personal interaction with the client during the review process that helps you understand your client's priorities and shows your focus on the client's success.

Keep in mind that the client always wants to know the one thing: "What's in this for me? How will this benefit me personally?" It's not that the other person is selfish; it's just the client's responsibility to view his or her job that way. By focusing on the client's priorities, you gain credibility and respect.

The client review process is different from the written anonymous-type survey that is completed by the client and returned with no further feedback. Management-level employees, rather than some third-party survey company, will conduct the research and gather the client's feedback.

Someone other than those involved in the current project should conduct the interview. Management should be involved, giving the process added significance. It demonstrates to the client a high level of commitment from management. The purpose and focus is on showing commitment to the client and on gaining commitment to your company from the client, thus establishing the bases of a long-term relationship.

The client review process is focused more on how the client feels about your company and how it operates, and less on measuring client satisfaction on a specific project. Most importantly, a personal review offers the opportunity to see body language and facial expression. Facial expressions and body language can sometimes say much more than words. The client appreciates the personal connection and immediate feedback. If done correctly, the review will show clients that you are focused on their personal success and are committed to their projects. It will create the perception that it was done for their benefit. Conducting a client satisfaction review in person makes this an important client-focused event which benefits your company's quality improvement process as well.

Preliminary Preparation for the Interview. When the decision is made to conduct a client review, follow these steps:

1. Determine who will make the initial contact and explain to the client the purpose of why you want to meet with him or her.
2. Tell the client that this process is a renewed commitment by your company for continuous improvement and you would like for him or her to be a part of that process.

3. Ask to make an appointment for one hour and then stick to the schedule unless the client prolongs it.

4. Let the client know the name and role of the other person you are bringing along.

5. Try to meet where there will be no distractions, away from phones and other people.

6. A few days prior to the appointment, send an e-mail with a list of the topics you will be discussing. Let the client know that no preparation is necessary on his or her part.

7. Assure the client that this is not necessarily to discuss specifics of his or her project, project managers, or any particular individual. Most people will be uncomfortable talking about an individual for fear of getting the person in trouble.

8. Make sure the client understands that you want to get his or her input on your company's overall service improvement process.

9. Before you arrive for your client review, complete as much information as possible ahead of time. This will help you become familiar with the client and projects that have been done in the past. Educate yourself on any previous history—particularly any issues or concerns that developed before.

10. You should know all the names of people that have been involved in previous projects, the length of the relationship, previous projects completed, the amount of revenue, the bid and contract type, and any previous issues. You should also be prepared to discuss any known future projects. By doing some preliminary information-gathering everyone is on the same page going in. The client feels that you are knowledgeable about his or her situation, company, and projects.

11. Take someone with you. It's difficult to ask questions, organize your thoughts, listen, and take notes all at the same time. Another person can help listen and take notes. Take notes consistently throughout

the conversation so that it does not appear that some facts are more important to you than others.

The Interview Process. There is a defined process and method for conducting successful client reviews and interviews:

1. Upon arrival:
      a. Put the client at ease and help organize his or her thoughts.
      b. Thank the client for his or her time and review why you are there.
      c. State how long it will take and confirm that the time meets his schedule.
      d. Explain how the information will be used, that long-term benefits for the client as well as your company will result from the information you gather. The information will be used to improve company processes to better meet client needs, improve quality, and customer service.
      e. Address the issue of confidentiality so that the client feels free to speak openly. Be careful here because rarely can you make an absolute promise, but you can assure the other person that this information is for internal use only and that you will obtain permission to use any quotes.
      f. Explain that you will personally manage issues that affect him or her.

2. Be professional but relaxed, using an informal but direct conversational tone.
3. Explain what you would like to discuss and review the questions that will be asked. The client should feel involved in the process as early as possible.
4. It is OK to let the client decide which questions to start with. If the client wanders into a different area while answering a question, listen for the significance of his or her remarks, but then direct the conversation *back* to where you were. If you skip ahead, you may miss valuable pieces of information.

5. Avoid leading or biased questions, and note that the sequencing of questions is important.

6. Questions should be open ended, positive, and asked one at a time, probing for details on each.

7. Try to remain neutral and avoid problem solving at this point. Make a note to come back to the issue later.

8. If you suspect potential controversial issues, begin by gathering facts and other light information first in order to establish a positive communication pattern.

9. Don't try to defend or solve issues during the interview. This is one reason to have those not involved in the current project conducting the interview.

10. Be a sponge. Just gather facts and then let the client know that you will get back with results and any changes that were made.

In any communication process, the most effective method of getting information is to ask the right questions. You will feel more at ease if you have prepared questions ahead of time. It also shows credibility and helps you maintain control when following a set format. You want to appear strong and in control.

During the conversation, give the client positive nonverbal feedback, such as leaning forward, nodding, and smiling. Keep the energy high by keeping the client focused, showing you are interested in everything he or she has to say.

Keeping the client focused is also a way of making the best use of time. If the client starts to wander off course, you'll need to determine if the information can be valuable for understanding his or her needs and concerns. But then just direct the client back with the next question.

Remember you are there to listen more than talk. Use open-ended questions, but avoid making the client feel interrogated. Spend some time probing for the depth of what he or she just said. Remember to be a sponge, and don't try to problem-solve at this point. Let the client continue with his or her train of thought so that you can gather as many facts as possible before responding. Wait until the person runs out of steam before going on to the next question.

Ask the Right Open-Ended Questions. Here are a few questions that can be used to gather useful information from either existing or previous clients. These questions can be used in any situation, but were designed for the client-review process. It works well to build a form that contains the questions right for your firm, leaving room for you to enter notes when the client answers. Don't hand the client the form to be completed, because you will need to probe and listen for additional information.

Don't ask all of these at one time, but choose those that apply. You don't want the client to feel interrogated! The goal is to get him or her talking. Ask questions in a natural way, listen, and then clarify for understanding.

1. What could we have done better? (You'll use this question many times, depending on what is being discussed.)
2. Did we respond to you in a timely manner? Is there room for improvement? (Spend sufficient time on each question so that you know you have gathered as much information as possible surrounding that subject. Use this saying often: "Tell me more about that." It works in all situations.)
3. Did we provide effective innovations and solutions?
4. Did we deliver in the time frame that you required?
5. Did we complete tasks within budget while effectively managing the scope of work?

6. Did we understand your requirements on your last project?

7. Do our deliverables consistently meet your requirements?

8. Did we provide appropriately skilled personnel necessary to do the job? (Even if the client answered this question while discussing one of the others, ask it again. You may learn additional information.)

9. Do our contracting practices make it easy to do business with us?

10. Do we provide value for the price paid?

11. And after any question, it's always an appropriate time to again ask, "How could we have done better?"

The client may answer some of these questions while responding to another question, so just note the information. You can come back later for clarification or to expand for more detail if necessary. These types of questions open the discussion to many things that might be on the client's mind, so give them individual time to gather thoughts. Encourage more detail by using probing questions such as, "Can you tell me more about that?" Remember to probe and clarify after each response until you feel that you have gathered as much information as possible.

Here are some other questions to use that can provide insight into how you rank in the client's eyes against your competition. If the client does not have an answer to any of these, don't force it; just go on to the next question and come back to it later if it feels right.

12. We would like your honest feedback on where we rank in the industry.

13. What differentiates us from our competitors?

14. How do you compare our company against our competitors? Who does it better?

15. Is there a company outside of the industry (i.e.: UPS, McDonalds, US Post Office) that you would compare us to? Why?

It's important to hear such honest feedback in order to understand where you rank in the industry.

How to answer "What's in it for me"?

1. What changes or improvements on our part would make your job easier?
2. What specifically can we do to help your organization attain a competitive advantage?
3. What trends do you see in your industry that may affect the services that you will need in the future?
4. Tell me about the challenges you will face in the next twelve months.

Good closing questions:

1. Do you have any other suggestions or concerns that need to be discussed?
2. What else can we do to demonstrate our ongoing commitment to continuous performance improvement?
3. What else do we need to know?
4. A great final question is *"How often should I follow up with you?"* Let the client tell you how often to call; it will also tell you how much attention he or she requires.

Asking open-ended questions encourages the client to talk. Try to avoid yes/no questions. Make sure you are listening more than talking; the client should be talking at least 70 percent of the time. Ask the questions that guide the conversation, and then *listen*. Remember, the client always wants to know one thing: "What's in it for me? How will this benefit me personally?" So you will want to summarize at the end, and again explain how this process benefits the client by helping your firm better understand the individual's needs and the company's needs.

Active Listening. One of the most important aspects of communication is listening skills. You should be listening at least 70 percent of the time.

What are you listening for? You are listening for the facts, but you need to understand what's behind the facts. Read the person's body language and respond naturally. It is important to understand what the client means when they talk about problems they are having, their need for innovation, their desire for low cost, and how they value experience. When you are interacting face-to-face you can probe for additional clarification.

What's behind the words that explain the client's situation? Is there a crisis? Is the client planning ahead to new projects? Now is the time to go back and clarify by linking your question about something that the client stated as a concern or goal: "You mentioned low cost; what is the concern?" There again you could just say, "Can you tell me more about your cost concerns?"

Keep going until you are sure the client has stated, and you have clarified, his or her complete concerns and thoughts. Then summarize and verify what the client said by asking, "Do I understand your goals and concerns?" Review action items that you will be addressing personally.

Following the answer to each question, you can dig deeper by using phrases such as these:

- Please tell me more about that.
- What do you mean by…?
- In what way…?
- How else…?
- Help me understand….
- What specifically…?
- How would you like…?

Then you can go further with those responses to gather as much information as possible about points that are important to the client. Now you can see why you need at least an hour for this interview process.

In any situation, listening to a client can be either active or passive. Knowing what to listen for is the part of the client-maintenance process that needs the most attention. Listening requires a tremendous amount of emotional involvement and sincerity. Make sure you are leaning slightly forward and making easy eye contact. Asking clients what they want and how they want it is a way to show that you care about their needs. It is vital to building a loyal client base where your company is viewed as a trusted advisor. However, clients will not care until they are sure that you care. The process of active listening and genuine concern for the client's thoughts helps to show the client that you care and in the process your company will become their trusted advisor.

Ask for a Testimonial Letter. When your client interview is completed, and assuming that most of the responses have been positive, ask the client for a testimonial letter. You might offer to write it and send it to him or her for changes or additions. The client can then print it company letterhead. This makes it easy for clients to agree because they will not be required to start from scratch or put a great deal of effort into compiling the letter. Complete this as soon as possible after your discussion and let them know when to expect it.

Continue to Communicate. It's incredibly important to continue to communicate with clients on their terms. Stay visible to them as much as possible. Otherwise they may begin to feel that they are being taken for granted. Good client communication is not a one-time event but a continuous process. Communication is such a complex activity—particularly in business. Your main objective should be to talk with your clients in a way that builds a solid and trusting relationship and to gain information that helps you to grow and improve the company. Do not assume that you know the answers. Only when you hear and understand what your clients want can you be sure that you are meeting their expectations and creating customer loyalty.

Key Concepts in this Chapter

1. Good communication skills are learned, it seldom comes natural. Effective communication can make the difference between having a successful career and happiness, and a stress filled life.
2. Communication skills can create client loyalty and help you to understand their needs.
3. Different types of people require different methods of communication.
4. In this chapter we discuss interviewing existing clients in order to determine what improvements can be made in existing work and to uncover potential future projects.
5. The ability to manage controversial issues well, requires special communication skills.
6. Active listening skills should be considered part of the communication process.

10

BODY LANGUAGE

Body language is discussed a number of places throughout this book because understanding the language of the body is a very important part of communicating with other people. Whether speaking with clients or coworkers, your ability to read them and respond appropriately helps to manage conversations in a positive way. It is also helps you to make sure the words you speak are coming across as you intended.

Have you ever walked into a room and known what was going on before anybody spoke? Have you watched somebody on a cell phone and known the general tone of the conversation by the body language? People react to what they see—not what you say. Body language is the message you interpret from the other person and helps you to read the meaning of words that are spoken.

It's Not All Words. Did you know that communication is not just the words that are spoken? Communications is:

  7 percent the words spoken

  35 percent tone and inflections of the voice

  55 percent body language. It is yours and the other person's:

> Appearance
>
> Posture
>
> Gestures
>
> Eye contact
>
> Expressions

3 percent is the surroundings and background noise

When there is a discrepancy between the words spoken and the body language it creates miscommunication. We have the feeling that something is not right, and generally end up not believing what the other person is saying to be true. It is also the reason that it is sometimes difficult for us to like another person. Have you ever heard yourself thinking, "I don't why, but I just have a hard time liking Mary—there's just something about her." It may be that her body language does not match the words she speaks.

Body language is not an exact science, and there are many details about nonverbal communication that are interesting to learn but are not necessary for a basic understanding. Keep in mind that all body language interpretation must be based on the context and circumstances of the situation. For Business Development conversations, it can be helpful to have an understanding of a few common body language communications:

- **Smile**. A smile is a universal language. It says, "I'm glad to see you" or "I want to be your friend."
- **Eye Contact.** Easy eye contact creates the impression that you are engaged and interested in what is being said and that you are interested in the other person. If eye contact is not good—looking around the room or gazing into the distance while speaking—the impression is that you would rather be someplace else, or that you may be insecure, or shifty, or not interested.
- **How to Shake Hands.** Your handshake is body language that makes a critical first impression, particularly in business. The per-

fect handshake is one that shows connection to the other person. Step toward the person, lean slightly forward, look into the eyes. Extend your right hand and introduce yourself while pumping slightly two to three times. The web between the thumb and first finger should connect. It's best to keep the handshake neutral so that both your hand and the other person's hand are in the same position. Use an easy, comfortable grip; make sure to shake your entire arm, not just the wrist and fingers. A handshake that is too strong and held too long can be interpreted as controlling or wishing to dominate. A wimpy handshake could be interpreted as a sign of weakness. A wimpy handshake, no eye contact, slumped posture, and shifting body weight will be perceived as insecure and incompetent. Such body language can potentially ruin a business image and any chance of forming a meaningful relationship.

- **Crossed Arms** indicate that the individual is distrustful, closed off, or restrained. If a person has arms crossed and is turned toward the door, you can be sure they do not want to participate in the conversation. If someone has arms crossed and is leaning away from the speaker, he or she probably does not believe, or does not want to believe, what is being said. If someone is leaning toward you, making good eye contact, and has an open body stance, you can assume that he or she is interested in what you have to say.
- **Head Touching**. When people scratch their head or look confused—they probably are. They need additional information or clarification.
- **Eyes.** Covering (or rubbing) the eyes may be an indication that the person does not like what he or she hears or sees and does not want to be involved. Or, the other person may position something between you as a barrier, which is another indication he or she is not comfortable with the conversation.

- **Neck**. Touching the neck usually means that there is more to this than is openly discussed. There could be underlying issues that have not come to the surface. Be patient and wait for the person to share additional information that will give you a clue. Or, if you are the one speaking you will need to clarify.

- **Face.** Touching the face, particularly the mouth, may be a give-away that this person is uncertain about they are saying or may be lying. It may also indicate that he or she feels the same to be true about what you are saying.

- **Voice**. A rapid, high-pitched voice indicates uncertainty or insecurity. Rapid breathing also indicates uncertainty.

- **Hands on the Hips** is either a sign of impatience, confrontation or defiance…or maybe the other person is just resting his or her back or just habitually stands this way.

- **Finger Tapping** can indicate the person is impatient or is ready for a change.

- **Tight Hands**. Hands that are tightly clenched or obviously nervous may be agitated or irritated.

- **Posture** is an indication of an individual's feelings about the situation. An upright strong posture indicates that the person is sure of what he or she is saying and confident about the situation. A slumped posture tells you the person is uncertain or is not telling the complete truth.

Everybody communicates differently, so you may need to make some allowances. Verify what you believe you see in another's body language by asking for feedback. You may be able to clarify your message, or theirs, to avoid a misunderstanding.

What to Do About Negative Body Language. There may be a time when you receive negative body language and find it necessary to change the attitude of the other person. An effective method is to mimic, or mirror, that behavior to show a connection with where the individual is currently. Then slowly change to the behavior that fits the reaction you want. This must be done slowly and with caution. If the other person catches on to what you are doing he or she may feel insulted and embarrassed—nobody likes to feel controlled. By mirroring or mimicking another's body language cues, on a subconscious level the other person feels you are connected to his or her thoughts and feelings.

For example, if the other person assumes a position that indicates resistance, such as arms crossed and looking at the nearest exit, mirror that behavior. Slowly cross your arms and speak in confident calm tones, and ask questions that help you regain control. Then, slowly uncross your arms and let your arms fall to your sides, or sit comfortably with your hands naturally in your lap. If you've done your job well, your companion will follow suit. Now your job is to figure out why the other person has negative feelings and change that attitude.

When someone is tapping fingers or shaking a leg anxiously, the person does not like what is going on. Just mimic the behavior in a subtle way and then switch to a more receptive and calm pose. Make sure you are focused on the other person and show agreement to what is being said by making eye contact, nodding, and showing interest. Nodding is important to show understanding and agreement, but should be done in moderation and when appropriate.

When your companion changes to a more positive demeanor, you will know that you are one step closer to engaging the person completely. All this may sound contrived, but if you catch it early enough in the conversation you can still manage to turn this into a more positive situation. The trick is to stay in the moment instead of racing ahead to what you want to say. Until the other person feels a comfortable connection with you, your words will fall on deaf ears anyway.

Likability. Have you ever noticed that it is just easier to like some people more than others, but you're not sure why? It may have something to do with their body language. Notice the next time you are around people that everybody clearly seems to like. They don't worry about how they look and they never seem to be concerned with power or control.

They step toward you and appear to be genuinely interested in learning all about you. They may lean in slightly and look you in the eye. At the moment you are in the conversation, they behave as if you are the only person in the room. They ask questions that show an interest in knowing more about you or whatever you just said. Likable people are not afraid of tasteful touch—for some reason it's OK when they touch you, because you sense that it means they care about you. Touch breaks down natural barriers and decreases the distance between two people, which is a key component of being liked.

The next time you find yourself in a situation that requires understanding of another person, notice the body language, combine it with the words being spoken, and respond accordingly.

Key Concepts in this Chapter

1. Body language is a form of communication and is about fifty-five percent of how humans communicate.
2. In this chapter we discussed:
    a. How to understand and read the other person's true meaning.
    b. How to read and turn around negative body language.
    c. How to make sure you are coming across as intended.
    d. How to be viewed as a likeable person.

11

BUILDING A PROPOSAL

Proposals—we either love them or hate them. Either way, almost everyone in the business of providing professional services is responsible for writing or participating in the development of proposals. Generally, proposals are in response to Requests for Proposals (RFPs) or Requests for Qualifications (RFQs) from an interested client.

If you think of the process more in terms of developing solutions for your clients, it makes pulling together a winning proposal much easier, and it is more meaningful to clients. An effective proposal strategy succeeds in influencing the client's ultimate decision about who will be awarded the work. Know the client and understand the company's issues before beginning a proposal. By understanding the client, and using the proper questioning techniques in earlier meetings, you can uncover issues and concerns that can be used to influence the selection in your favor. Hopefully this was done before receiving the RFP, because the client will usually not be permitted to talk with you about this particular RFP once it is published.

Your proposal is a *sales document*. It should be informative and give the requested information, but it should give the information in such a way as to be persuasive. However, keep in mind that the proposal becomes part of the client's contract and is called the *offering*. This is why it must be completely accurate. In your enthusiasm to win the project, make sure that the truth does not become stretched out of shape. Promote your qualifications so as to sell, but do so truthfully; otherwise, it may come back to bite you one day.

Your company image is at stake when it comes to proposals. Much attention must be paid to the quality, editing, and production of your company's proposals. Make sure the pages are easy to read, that they follow a consistent theme throughout, that graphics fit, and the editing is perfect. Make sure all information is relevant to the RFP and that specific instructions in the RFP are followed to the letter. When all elements are presented perfectly, then you are assured of a high-quality professional document that enhances your company's image.

Problems with Developing Proposals. Take steps to mitigate the problems that seem to consistently plague every proposal developed. The following are a few common problems that seem to happen during the proposal development process:

> **Procrastination**: The solution to procrastination is to begin work on the proposal as soon as you know it is coming out. Get as much completed as possible ahead of time, even if you know you have plenty of time before the due date.

> **The "Oops" factor**: If a key element is missing that is required to submit, and it is not discovered until the day before it's due, the proposal effort becomes somebody's unnecessary emergency. The solution is to jointly develop a compliance checklist and assign responsibilities. Assign one person to monitor and to take responsibility for the process.

Indecisiveness: There may be difficulty in making a decision about which project write-ups will be used, and the people who will be assigned to work on the project. Make those decisions as soon as possible so that everyone on the proposal development team knows the organizational chart that is being proposed to the client.

Lack of direction: This can be very frustrating. Every proposal effort needs someone to drive the process and provide direction. When there is no direction or strategy, everyone begins doing their own thing. Many times a person or group says they have everything under control, or it may all be happening in one person's head. Then it is discovered at the last minute that not enough has been done. The solution to this problem is to have a strong proposal manager who understands the importance of working with a plan and keeping the team focused.

Time Constraints: Stressful time constraints happen when one person tries to control the proposal until time has run out. Another thing that can happen is assigning the brunt of writing to project managers with no consideration for their existing workload. The right solution is better planning and communication as early in the process as possible.

Get It Right the First Time: The goal should be to get the proposal development effort right the first time and thus avoid endless rewrites. Rewrites and redirection can be frustrating and big time wasters. Getting it right the first time takes communication and planning. The amount of early planning has a direct impact on the quality of the final submittal and the efficiency of the team. Better planning greatly minimizes the stress level and proposal development costs.

Follow a Structure. To be able to focus on writing winning proposals, your company must have a structure in place that is repeated with each proposal effort. A structured process assures that a proposal is of the highest quality, responds to the RFP, and enhances the overall experience for the participants. There is nothing more stressful than trying to pull together a proposal at the last minute. Throwing something together at the last minute will almost guarantee that the quality of the submittal will be below standard.

Analyze the Opportunity. To begin, objectively analyze the opportunity. This is a formal systematic process for determining whether or not to propose on the project. This task should start even before the RFP is issued, because you should have been talking to the client who would have told you about it. Finding a posted RFP and "taking a shot at it" is generally a waste of resources. The reality is that even if the project is perfect for your skill set, you will have about a 5 percent chance of winning when responding to a solicitation that you found on the Web. This is especially true when you've had no previous interaction with the client. Make sure there is a relationship or at least some meaningful interaction has taken place with the project owner before you even consider going after it.

Next, develop an initial strategy that lays the groundwork for developing a winning proposal. When the RFP is received, the response process might look like this:

1. Read through it at least twice with a highlighter and identify *client and project issues.* Look for any unusual requests or instructions (legal requirements, bonding, contractual items, etc.).
2. Develop a client profile to understand how much is known about them.
3. Develop a competitor profile to help identify how to differentiate from the competition.

4. Assess company capabilities. Do you have the resources and the time to put together a quality winning proposal?

5. Identify potential risks and how they can be mitigated.

6. Estimate the cost to pursue. What's it going to cost you to develop a response? How much profit will you make? Is it worth it?

Putting together a quality proposal can be very expensive, and if there is not a definable reason to propose on this project, then consider passing on this one. Never submit a proposal as a marketing ploy—it sends the wrong message. If you decide not to go after an RFP that was sent to you directly, let the client know your reasoning. He or she will appreciate your honesty and will keep you in mind for future projects that might be a better fit.

The Go/No-Go Decision. There are many things to be considered before spending the resources to go after a project. The first and most important decision to be made in the proposal development process is the Go/No-Go decision. This is the step that can greatly affect your proposal win rate. Evaluate your existing proposal win rate. Is your win rate good compared to others in your industry? Making the right proposal decisions can be a good way to control Business Development costs.

Go/No-Go decisions should be based on fact and not on emotional attachments or the excitement at having received an RFP. Here are a few questions to ask your team:

1. What has previously been done to position you to win this project?
2. Do you know the client well enough to be able to identify at least five key issues of concern, or drivers surrounding the project?
3. Do you know the selection committee well enough to know what the "hot buttons" are for making this decision?

4. Is this project using your firm's core competency? Is it in your target market? Do you have resources available or will you need to team with another firm?

5. Do you know the competition? Is it possible that it is wired for someone else and this RFP was issued in order to obtain proposals to satisfy outside requirements or to price shop?

6. Are you certain that the client actually has budgeted money for the project? Or could this be a fishing expedition?

7. Is this a client that you want to work with? Will the project be profitable?

8. Would the effort help your company to grow strategically?

If you know the client well enough and have asked the right questions, the answers to these questions will have come up in conversation along the way before you ever receive the RFP. Answering positive to 50 percent of these agrees with a *Go* decision; otherwise, do additional research before making a final decision. There may occasionally be other subjective factors to consider such as; Is this a new market sector that you are targeting? Have you been watching for an opportunity to place your credentials in front of this prospective client? Are you expected to submit a proposal in order to get in line for the next project? These are not good reasons to propose or bid, but may be considered in certain situations.

Working through the Go/No-Go decision guide may appear to be additional work but it will create a greater sense of clarity and assurance that the right decision has been made. Making proposal response decisions will not always be cut and dried, but with a systematic approach it becomes more realistic. The following is a suggested format for the Go/No-Go decision guide:

Go/No-Go Decision Guide

Please answer all questions completely.

1. Client Name:
   a. Name of the Project:
2. Proposal Manager:
   a. Proposal Team:
   b. Department:
3. Teaming Partners and their roles:

   _____   _____

   _____   _____

4. Source of the RFP _____
5. Client selection committee members:

   _____   _____

   _____   _____

6. Does the work fit our strategic plan?   ☐ Yes   ☐ No
7. Probability of winning (%)? _____%
8. Competitive advantage _____
9. Scoring criteria in RFP _____
10. Time and resources available for preparation of a quality proposal?
11. Competition—any shoo-ins? ☐ No   ☐ Yes Who? _____
12. Pre-marketing completed? What and how long ago? _____
13. New client: ☐ Yes ☐ No Extension of existing client work? ☐ Yes ☐ No
14. Estimated revenue for this project:
15. Special requirements that can take additional time:
    (i.e., conceptual plan, GIS maps, CAD drawings, etc.)
16. Proposal deadlines: Mailing date ____Actual proposal due date _____
17. Time considerations of the team _____
    (e.g., vacations, other proposals in progress, other responsibilities that might interfere with this effort, etc.)

18. **Final Decision:**   ☐ No-Go   ☐ Go
     ☐ Project set-up form completed
     ☐ Project folder created
     ☐ Proposal team available to attend pre-proposal meeting

Pre proposal meeting date _____

Once the Go/No-Go decision has been made, the proposal development process will look something like this:

1. Select a *proposal manager*
2. Request proposal/SOQ number
3. Send RFP to contracts administration for review
4. Determine proposed project team
5. Assign proposal *production manager*
6. Assign *technical writing team*
7. Contact review *red team* to be on alert
8. Prepare outline of scope and requirements
9. Develop timeline working backward from due date
10. Assemble any teaming partners and gather information from them
11. Complete draft proposal
12. Submit for red team review
13. Make edits and revision
14. Submit for final review
15. Finalize and produce
16. Send finished proposal via predetermined method

Managing the Process. Planning and managing a proposal effort should be carried out as seriously as you would any other important project. Give yourself enough time to do a good job. Start right away, even if you have plenty of time before the due date. Set a drop-dead due date for content that is *at least four days* before the actual due date. Remember to consider holidays, weekends, and possible weather constraints.

Roles and Responsibilities

Each member of the proposal team will have a different set of responsibilities but they must work together as a team to accomplish the challenging task of pulling together a winning proposal.

Proposal Manager. Select one person to be the proposal manger. It usually works best if the proposal manager is not the project manager for the job. Different skill sets are required for making sure all the components of a proposal response are being done and that all deadlines are met. The effort should be managed by one person whose primary job is to encourage creativity in responding to the RFP and to direct responsibilities. This person will also be the one who will keep everyone on schedule. They should keep a running list of action items that is reviewed each morning.

The proposal manager assembles a core proposal team, sets up a meeting or conference call, and assigns roles and responsibilities. The team will proceed to plan the development of the proposal. The amount of planning that is done up front will determine the resulting quality of the final submittal. The proposal manager is responsible for communication and organization during the proposal development process.

The proposal manager should be a technical person with previous experience in the type of work outlined in RFP. Not required, but desired, is familiarity with the client and the industry sector.

The proposal manager:

- Submits the RFP and contracts to the legal team for evaluation
- Assembles the proposal team
- Alerts management and the red team
- Makes final decisions regarding resumes and projects
- Manages the process much like any other project
- Encourages creativity
- Directs responsibilities
- Clearly defines roles and responsibilities
- Keeps everyone on schedule according to the timeline

- Ensures any addenda are recorded, addressed, and included in the final document
- Makes sure document arrives to the client on time

Production Manager. This person is responsible for a quality document completed according to the timeline. Production management is generally the marketing department's responsibility and the manager should be someone who is familiar with methodologies needed to produce quality documents. The production manager should not be the person that will manage the proposal process. These are two different functions.

The production manager's job is to assemble and edit the document, concentrating on quality, formatting, and the overall appearance of the proposal. Once set, items such as the format, schedule, and the proposal process are not open for discussion; any questions or debates about them can be counterproductive. Creative discussions need to be focused on the response itself—not the production process.

The production manager:

- Develops outline of RFP requirements
- Develops timeline
- Develops compliance checklist
- Develops template of draft response from previous proposals and other available resources
- Edits document, looking for:
    - o   Grammar and spelling, proper use of words, etc.
    - o   Consistent with company style format
    - o   Clarity of message
    - o   Visual impact—does it have the right message?
    - o   Does it meet standards for logos, formatting, etc.?

- o Is the page layout consistent?
- o Does it use the language of client's industry?
- o Is the design of the entire document consistent and easy to read and follow?
- Ensures that the final document is addressed to the correct person and arrives in plenty of time—according to the RFP instructions.
- Tracks proposal documents as the various technical professionals submit them

The Technical Response Team. The proposal manager then selects the rest of the team that will be involved in the technical response. In addition to the proposal manager and production manager, the response team should be based on the requirements of the solicitation. This might consist of the project manager, the technical expert, the Business Development lead, marketing and graphics personnel, and teaming partners. After everyone has read and studied the RFP, and possibly attended a site tour for the project, the team then will proceed to develop a strategy for the proposal response.

Example of Proposal Development Worksheet—attach to inside of working folder.

Proposal Development Work Plan

Project Name

Proposal Number: Date:

Proposal Manager:

Production Manager:

RFP Distribution List:

    1. _____

    2. _____

    3. _____

    4. _____

Client Issues and Concerns:

    1. _____

    2. _____

    3. _____

    4. _____

Who		RFP Section	What	When	completed

Teaming partner information: _____

Schedule/timeline for completion: _____

Address for delivery—person responsible? _____

The team must:

- Define the scope of services
- Review the terms and conditions
- Begin to develop initial cost estimates
- Complete a client profile, a competitor profile, and a client's key issue analysis
- Build a compliance checklist from the requirements listed in the RFP
- Develop a proposal outline
- Develop a milestone schedule
- Read the RFP again for questions to be submitted for clarifications to the issuer of the RFP if allowed. There is usually a cutoff date for questions.

During the proposal process, the entire team needs to be in constant communication with the proposal manager. Everyone needs to know if one or more elements appear to be holding up the process and determine how best to compensate so that the proposal schedule does not fall behind.

Before any writing takes place, the core proposal team should get together in an interactive atmosphere and storyboard the proposal effort using the client's key issues. The proposal team will determine a strategy, complete an outline, and will then make assignments before beginning to write the proposal. Once the proposal draft is complete, a red team reviews the draft, and revisions are made based on those comments. Management should be involved in the process as early as possible because they will need to approve the proposal before it is submitted to the client. The important thing is to know *where* you're going before beginning to write anything!

Red Team Review. Every proposal should have a red team review that consists of at least a member of the management team and a technical peer who is not involved in proposal process. They should begin with a critique of the draft proposal. They will read it as though they are the client and then make suggestions to the proposal team for changes, clarifications, or additions. It is good to meet and have a team discussion that revolves around the "win" theme to be sure the changes fit the original intent determined in the planning stage.

The red team review will emulate the client. Using the compliance checklist generated by the technical response team early in the planning process, the red team will check for:

- accuracy
- compliance
- completeness
- readable text
- information is properly weighted to the selection criteria
- responsiveness to the RFP
- tailored message comes across—not as boilerplate or stock verbiage
- benefit statements in every part
- graphics make sense for this project and are in the right place in the proposal
- it tells your story—there is clarity of a winning theme
- persuasiveness—leaves no question as to why your firm should be chosen for the project

Address Client Issues and Concerns. Highlighting client issues and providing your solutions are what will help you to develop a winning proposal strategy. In order to develop a proposal that will separate you from the competition, you must have a winning strategy and an effective theme based on client benefits for this proposal.

In order to determine a theme, the team should brainstorm to find issues and concerns that they know the client has on this project, and present solutions to each. A client issue or concern is a high-value need, or an obstacle, or anything that is important to the client related to this project. Quality of work is a given and will be expected from everyone. It must be addressed, but is not what will differentiate you from the competition.

Decide on a Proposal Theme. As early as possible in the proposal development process, identify a proposal theme that highlights your strategy, and then stick with it throughout the writing of the proposal. Begin each section with a theme statement that is focused on each client issue and your proposed solution, along with the benefit and proof statements.

Show innovative solutions that make your approach unique, and then elaborate on the benefits of using the solution you are suggesting. This can be done by carefully choosing the proof in the form of project descriptions about similar projects and discussing how they pertain to this particular project.

The Win Theme. Client needs will determine the "win" theme for the proposal. Many firms have a set way that they promote themselves without regard for client needs. You will have a much better chance of winning the work if you will remember that you don't choose your win theme—the client does.

Use your knowledge of the client and his or her situation, and evaluate the RFP or solicitation for possibilities. Your winning theme must be based on specific client needs. Most ideas will be centered on one of the following, and a win theme might use the descriptive words to build up the proof:

- Experience: Expertise, Proven, Tested, Quality
- Capabilities: Unique Functionality, Speed, Ease of Execution
- Trust: Competency, Security, Support
- Organizational: Strength, Reputation, Familiarity with Organization, Positioning

- Relationship: Positioning, Partnerships, Commitment, Corporate Alignment
- Platforms: Methodologies, Processes, Training

Most purchasing decisions originate from the emotional side of the brain. The left side (analytical side) of the brain will justify that decision. You must locate the wants that control the client's emotional side and prove how you can best meet those wants.

Find where your strengths intersect with client priorities. Show how your firm is unique in its ability to address the client's issues. Knowing client issues and concerns requires that you will have talked with the client before this point. Even if the RFP spells out everything the company wants to see in the response, you need to have a clear understanding of the significance of this project to the client in order to be able to put together a meaningful proposal. You want to look below the surface of what's contained in the RFP and present your benefit statements that connect with the client's issues. This is where you gain a competitive advantage and can play up your strengths in relation to the competition's weaknesses.

Build a Client Issues List. In the team brainstorming session, build a client issues worksheet that lists each concern or issue and how you might respond to them. Show the benefit of using your solution for the client, and show the proof in the form of a project write-up about similar projects and expertise. This proposal exercise can be taken a step further by addressing how you think the competition might respond and countering that in your proposal. An easy way to do that is with a T-chart.

Compare Strengths and Weaknesses. A T-chart compares your strengths and weaknesses to those of the competition for each issue. Just make a T that covers a big Post-It sheet. Put the client issue at the top and then list your company's strengths for this opportunity on one side of the chart and your weaknesses on the other. Do the same process for the competition. You can use the T-chart to help highlight your strengths and mitigate weaknesses in the proposal. It can also be used to neutralize your competition's strengths and to enhance their weaknesses. This process helps to clarify where you need to focus your skills of persuasion and what to use as your winning theme when developing your proposal strategy.

Use Benefits Statements. The benefits statement tells clients what your solutions will *do* for them. Benefits should always be tied back to the issue—it's what the client actually buys. For example, when people say they are going to the store to buy a drill, the drill is not really what they want. It is the hole that it makes! Sell the benefit in your proposal.

Every benefit statement should have a proof statement connected to it. The proof is what you offer as examples of having provided similar solutions on other projects. The proof is necessary in order to gain credibility and the client's confidence and trust. It may be as simple as demonstrating how a similar project successfully provided a needed solution. Showing your understanding of the project, and offering ideas for solutions that will benefit the client, are how to create a winning proposal.

Make Assignments. Assign authors to write their assigned sections based on the T-charts and a strategy which is designed to differentiate you from the competition. You want to be able to clearly state in several different ways why you should be chosen for this project. Infuse compliance to the RFP, and your strategy for addressing client issues and concerns, but also tell your story.

Create a Storyboard. Grab attention by telling a story. An excellent planning tool for developing a winning proposal is the development of a storyboard. The storyboard is created before any writing begins. Use the client issues list and the T-charts to help develop your story. It becomes the draft for the proposal, and also provides a template to keep everyone on the same track. The storyboard keeps the process from getting bogged down and happening only in one person's head. This is a common problem when one person takes control of the proposal effort; if that person should get sidetracked, the process can get messy and stressful for the others on the team.

Storyboarding saves time, saves rework, and helps writers develop solutions that are on target to the client's problems and issues. When you tell a story, people are more likely to remember the solutions that you offer. Storyboarding ensures that your winning proposal will be based around the client's key issues or concerns. When the client's issues and concerns are accurately identified, the storyboard uses those issues to form the theme that will be used throughout the proposal.

Your story is based on your specific approach to addressing how you will solve the client's key issues of concern. It's *what and how*—or the benefits and proof statements. As everyone participates in the brainstorming process, it begins to generate ideas that can build off each other. Building a storyboard may sound like extra work up front, but it will actually save a lot of time, effort, and money in the long run. It can also serve as a guide for the executive summary and the cover letter.

For each section of the proposal, list the issues and topics that must be addressed. Begin developing solutions for each, looking for opportunities to be innovative, and giving examples or proof to support the approach. Check for completeness and credibility of the story. More discussion may be needed to make sure the reader will understand how you plan to provide solutions to the problem. Gather input from others on the team.

The amount of time spent planning and storyboarding ultimately determines the ease with which the proposal gets pulled together and the final quality of the submittal. How extensive your storyboard becomes depends on the size and requirements of the opportunity. Here is an example of how a storyboard might work.

Each section can be based on a client issue and begins with a two-sentence theme statement, which becomes the main topic of the section.

- Name a client issue or concern.
- Develop the *how and what* of each issue.
- State the *benefit* to the client of your solution or approach, and then provide *proof.*
- Answer *why* your company should be chosen.
- Imagine that the client is asking, "*So what?*" and continue to clarify.

It might look something like this:

> *Point 1—Cost Reduction Ideas* (an identified client concern from a previous discussion or as identified in the RFP). "Identify all ideas that could significantly lower client cost of service, cost of facilities, or cost of operations. Quantify the potential cost savings."

> The team then generates ideas for addressing the issue. Once that is done, the writer will use these ideas as a guide for writing a designated portion of the proposal. Continue doing the same with other issues and concerns on the list.

Storyboarding works great when you have a large proposal to produce, since large proposals can become overwhelming. Try using the walls of your conference room to post everything from your discussions (ideas, themes developed, etc.) and use that same room for review sessions. The wall becomes a mockup of the proposal—your storyboard. Large Post-it pads work best because they can be moved around without damage to the wall.

Make sure there is plenty of room to spread out. Having space makes it easier for peer reviewers to follow the checklist. Using a real wall allows several people access to the storyboard at the same time. The pieces can be moved around as discussions require. You might manage the storyboard via computer when there are multiple contributors in different locations. The key is to make it available to everyone working on the proposal.

You may want to schedule a dedicated proposal room so that everything can be left up. Put up the client issues worksheets, T-charts, the sections of the "win" strategy, the RFP, timetable or schedule that includes the due dates, and anything else that will be needed for reference. It is best if the storyboard wall is set up in sections that follow how your proposal is to be laid out. Appoint a person to manage the wall and keep everyone informed of changes. You may want to do this electronically but there is just something about having pieces of paper to move around that some people find helpful.

Cloud computing offers a method for all team members to access the same documents and information at the same time from various locations. Having simultaneous access allows several people to work from the same document, and significantly cuts down on rewriting time.

Templates Can Save Time. All proposals are different, but each type of project can follow the same general approach. Once you have a good general format or template, there is usually no need to reinvent the wheel each time. It goes without saying that the proposal should be 100 percent responsive to the RFP and should mirror the instructions in the RFP to the letter, but most proposals have the same or similar elements.

Common elements of most proposals include:

- Executive Summary
- Compliance Matrix
- Technical Approach
- Management Plan
- Personnel Resumes
- Organizational Charts and Responsibilities
- Project Experience
- Closing Summary

Building a template that addresses these common elements can reduce writing time and stress, and free up countless hours. Templates can act as the initial outline that is expanded to meet the specifics of the RFP. For a small company, personnel and corporate experience sections will generally be the same in every proposal.

You can develop several different standard versions around each of the services your company provides. Templates have generally been reviewed a number of times so quality is more consistent. Using them allows you the time to focus on meaningful text rather than recreating generic content. The more time reserved for refinements and modifications the better, especially for resumes and project descriptions. Focus on tailoring them exactly to the RFP.

Templates can also save you money. Think of it this way: It is possible for one page of proposal text written from scratch to take five hours or more. Using that estimate as a rough guide, a large proposal of one hundred pages could require as much as 500 hours. If you assume that technical professionals doing the writing can bill their time at $100 or more per hour, you could easily spend $50,000 responding to a major solicitation. Using templates can cut down on the time requirement by about 30 percent. Another cost savings is to make sure you have a very good chance of winning the project before you even begin.

Editing. Once the red team review is completed and the changes are incorporated, the document receives a final edit. Editing consumes a lot of time, so be sure to leave enough time in the schedule to edit and rewrite. Allow time to review the draft of each section write-up as it is completed. This should be done by someone other than the writer. The draft will then receive a final editing by a production staff professional. A great deal of time goes into editing and review of the document. Many proposal managers make the mistake of not leaving enough time for this final step.

Visuals. Using visuals can be a very powerful means of communication in a document, especially in a proposal that includes technical information. Including a visual in each section which fits the overall theme of the proposal can do a lot to help clarify and tell the story. Keep in mind that any visual or graphic must have a reason to be included. Make graphics simple and to the point, and always include captions and text as support for the visuals. The production manager or editors should make sure that the section's graphics and visuals sell your company's past experience. All graphics must be related to the client's issues and concerns.

The Executive Summary. Allow plenty of time for writing the executive summary. In some situations, the executive summary is the only piece of the proposal that gets read. It should be considered a very important part of the proposal effort and should reflect the theme and story that the proposal spells out in more detail. Sometimes high-level executives and purchasing-agent decision-makers will read only the executive summary; therefore this section should be tailored for that level of decision-maker. It should be short, preferably one page, less technical, and to the point.

Have a strong opening statement of why your firm is the best choice, and then briefly discuss the client issues, your solutions to those issues, the benefits, and proof of those benefits. End with a closing statement asking for the business. Asking for the business is sometimes the hardest thing to do.

A time efficiency note: The executive summary can be used in many ways other than in this proposal. It can be used as a handout at the short-list presentation and other places where a short write-up is needed about this opportunity.

Follow Up After Submittal. After submitting your proposal, the lead contact person contacts the client to make sure the proposal was delivered, and supplies any additional information as required. If it is not already known, the lead contact person might ask when the decision will be made and how you will be notified.

The team conducts a post-proposal analysis to identify lessons learned, both from the response of the client and also the proposal development process. The goal is to identify things that went well and things that could be done better next time.

After the Decision. Ask for a client debrief—whether you lose or win. Always do this because you can gain valuable information that could prove helpful next time. It's possible to gain more informative feedback from failure than from a win, and sometimes the pain of loss drives behavioral changes more quickly than winning.

Win or lose, conduct an interview with a member of the selection committee to determine the merits and shortcomings of your proposal. If you do not, you lose a great opportunity to enhance future proposal efforts. It also allows your company another opportunity to interact with the decision-maker and further the professional relationship.

Following *rejection*:

- Don't blame the client or decision-maker personally.
- Be empathetic and understanding to the individual. Control personal reactions such as headshaking or frowning.
- Take a position of wanting to learn—don't be defensive.
- Maintain a positive attitude. Ask, "Why did the winners win?" not "Why did we lose?"
- Demonstrate good active listening by using eye contact, nodding, and other positive body language.
- Pose carefully prepared open-ended questions (how, what, where) to gather beneficial feedback.
- These are suggested questions you might ask:
    o   How effective was our proposal?
    o   How was the quality of our proposal?
    o   Did the executive summary highlight key points?
    o   Was the proposal theme on track?
    o   Did we communicate an understanding of your needs?
    o   What were our competitive advantages?
    o   What benefits would you gain by hiring our firm in the future?
    o   Was material easy to find in the proposal?
    o   What did you like best about the winning proposal?
    o   Are there other projects coming up that might be a better fit for us?
    o   Are there others in the organization we should meet?
    o   What could we do differently next time?
    o   How was price a factor?
- Ask only one question at a time, and wait for a complete response before moving on to the next. Summarize the major points.
- Work to establish rapport for future projects.

- Allow the other person to outline the company's definition of quality.
- Let the other person talk about the types of working relationships desired.
- Learn how to position for future opportunities.
- Close with an optimistic discussion of future work.
- Ask how often you should be in contact.
- Always end with, "Is there anything else we should know?"

Follow up with a note thanking them for the opportunity and their time, and let them know that you look forward to future opportunities to work for the organization.

When a proposal is lost, price is seldom the true deciding factor—contrary to what most people think. Sure, that may be what the prospect told you, but most likely what the person is really saying is, "Everyone's proposal looked the same to us, so we went with the least expensive option." This generally happens when you are not able to show differentiation and prove the value that you can bring. Showing prospects how you are different and can solve their problems gets them emotionally attached to making a decision in your favor. The strength of your message and your ability to get prospects emotionally on your side will determine how often your proposal will be the winning proposal.

Following a *win*:

There are a number of reasons to ask for an interview following a win, some of them would be to:

- Determine level of communication the client desires.
- Learn why the project was awarded to you.
- Clarify expectations for the project.
- Allow the client to outline the definition of quality.

- Let the client talk about the types of working relationship desired.
- Learn how to position for future opportunities.
- Example questions:
  o What factors influenced the selection? (Listen carefully; these answers will tell you the priorities for the project.)
  o What do we have that other firms do not?
  o What qualities did they have that we do not?
  o What are your expectations for this project?
  o Are there any changes to the project from the RFP specifications?
  o What is the preferred method of communication (e-mail, phone, text) and how much?
  o Are there others we should meet?
  o Are there other projects coming up that we should be aware of?

Following the debrief interview, share the information with others in your firm—especially the proposal team—and determine a strategy for remaining in contact with the client for future opportunities.

Begin Preparations for the Short-List Presentation. When the proposal has been submitted, it is time start getting ready for the short-list presentation. Start right away. The team will prepare to deliver a presentation consistent with the proposal win strategy. Use the storyboard that was used for developing the proposal. Most of the work is already completed and there is no need to start over. Do not give the same proposal information in your short-list presentation, but do try to follow the same winning theme that was used in the proposal.

Planning Is the Key. The proposal development process need not be difficult when enough planning and strategy development takes place early in the process. Better planning helps you to easily build more persuasive winning proposals. Keep in mind that up-front planning helps to save time and to create better quality proposals that are based on providing solutions to the client's needs. With up-front planning, the proposal process can actually be fun and very rewarding!

Key Concepts in this Chapter

1. Developing proposals can be stressful unless planned properly.
2. Analyze the opportunity using a defined Go/No-Go decision procedure before beginning to write.
3. A clear process and reasons for writing the proposal makes the task easier.
4. Develop a timeline that leaves plenty of time at the end for review and edits.
5. Each person involved in the response effort has a different role to fill so make sure they understand their responsibilities.
6. A winning proposal will tell a story that is focused on client issues and concerns.
7. Always ask for a debriefing whether you win or not.

12

THE SHORT-LIST PRESENTATION

You made the short list! You've gone through the selling cycle—relationship-building, due diligence, and the proposal submissions. At this point you realize that the short-listed competitors are *all* well qualified. Some might even argue that once the invitation to interview is received, the playing field is completely level again.

Wow. After all that effort—a completely level playing field. Back to square one. You know you must now build a winning short-list presentation that somehow separates you from the competition.

The first thing to understand is that a short-list interview is simply a face-to-face communication. It is a job interview with decision-makers who expect to be sold on why they should choose you and your company for the project—instead of the other companies that also made the short list. There will be the additional challenge of performing this communication along with a group of your coworkers. Let's discuss strategy, structure, and style for giving a winning group presentation.

Strategy. As soon as the proposal is submitted, immediately begin to structure the short-list presentation while all the details of the project and the client's issues are still fresh on your mind. This is the time to decide who will participate, what their roles will be, what theme to use for the presentation, and which client issues will be addressed.

Set Up a Schedule. Once you receive the notification that you've made the short list, work backward from the due date, giving yourself plenty of time to rehearse at the end. Here is a good approach to planning the time necessary to do a good job of building a winning presentation:

1. Allow three to five days to develop the content of the presentation,
2. Two days for development of the images and visuals,
3. Two days for circulating the draft and getting management approval, and
4. Two days for rehearsal. Go through the presentation three or more times. It takes this long for people to feel comfortable with what they are going to say.

Plan Your Presentation. Think of the presentation as an oral executive summary. Executive summaries should excite readers and make them anxious to see more. Your presentation should do the same. It should get the clients interested in working with you—so interested that they can't imagine working with anyone else.

Structure. Determine a theme or main message. And, make everything you say and every graphic you use point to the theme. A presentation that revolves around a central message is easier to develop and deliver. From the audience's standpoint, it is much easier to listen to and understand. You will be able to control the listeners' attention more completely if you have a central theme which they can get interested in.

Determine what information to include and then prepare a presentation strategy that addresses and is focused on the buyer's topmost concerns. Don't say the same thing as was in the proposal but your theme needs to grow out of your proposal win strategy. It must be directly related to the information that the client wants most. If not, you are off target and the audience will drift away.

Take every opportunity to point out how your solution will benefit the client. Pepper your presentation with benefits, large and small. Provide highlights of your experience that prove your capabilities to provide the desired solution. You need to talk about what you will do and how you will do it—that's what they came to hear, and that's what they will pay for in the end. When you leave the room, what is it that you want them to remember? That is what you keep coming back to—your theme point.

When asked, the decision-makers will be very forthright with what they want to see at a short-list presentation. They will also tell you what they *do not* want to see. Some of the things they will want to see:

- They *do* like for presentations to be customized and specific to the project. They like for the project manager to do the majority of the presenting.
- They want clear straightforward language that adds information, but does not repeat the proposal.
- They expect the project write-ups, examples, and illustrations to be easy to follow and specific to their project.
- They don't like to see a group that is disorganized, provides generic information, or overuses visuals that are not specific.
- They want to see how the team interacts with each other. Nobody likes prima donnas or long-winded speakers.

Don't try to give them too much. The goal for the short-list interview is to give them a reason to select your company and the presenting team. You must convince them that your team is unique—one of a kind! In the interview, the evaluators are looking to answer two main questions: Can we work with these people? Should we trust them with our project?

The client already knows you are technically competent. That's why you are here. It is not about the technical work—it's about the people!

A few things to understand about the decision-makers at a short-list presentation:

- Many of the decision-makers do not come from technical backgrounds.
- Most of the panel members don't really want to be there.
- They have to listen to the same pitch on the same topic over and over.
- They're looking for a team they can trust and work with.

Help them. Think about where they're coming from and give them what they need to make the decision in your favor.

There is no need to tell them about your company again, including the history and all the information you told them in proposal. Don't waste time talking about the same thing you told them in the proposal; hopefully they will have already read that. In addition, don't say the same thing that all the other firms will say: "We are great and wonderful and we do quality work!" Everyone else is saying that. The client accepts the fact that you are good at what you do, or you would not be here—that's a given.

Focus On Your Strengths. Based on the information you gathered during the proposal preparation, and any additional information that might have been gathered since the proposal was submitted, choose a few key points that you know must be sold in order to win the job.

Organize your points and information into a logical sequence that fits the way the human brain selects, organizes, and interprets data. When listeners can understand the logic of an argument, they listen better and may be able to better internalize your key differentiators. A logical structure lends itself well to creative repetition of content throughout the presentation. Speakers can mark content for the audience as it flows through a logical structure by using statements such as, "First, I'm going to cover X, then Y, and then Z." Your listeners can relax into the pattern of the content and really absorb the main messages.

Choose points where your company can excel, and focus your presentation around these differentiators to build your unique strategy. Everything else will support those key points. The reason you pick just a couple of points at a time is because if you get too many points, the clarity never happens.

Tell them how you will solve *their* problems in a personal and creative way. The first words out of your mouth will lay the foundation for how the audience will perceive you and what you have to say for the rest of the presentation. Be confident and professional, but friendly and humble.

Begin your presentation with a clear purpose statement to help your audience focus on the key points you want them to remember. Simple phrases such as these are good:

- "Our objective today is to show you why our company is the best choice for the success of this project."
- "In the next thirty minutes, we're going to focus on three main topics."
- "What we see as the top four critical issues in completing this project are…"
- "We are excited about this project, and here is how we will resolve the problem."
- "This is how we will use our experienced team members to manage the project."
- "Here is our plan for doing all the work necessary within your expedited schedule."

It can be as simple as that. Phrase the opening statement so that all of the components of your approach are mentioned, and then follow with the details. Make your introductory remarks compelling. Say what you're going to say in a way that makes the listener think, "Well, that's certainly interesting. I wonder what other interesting things they have to say."

Next, discuss the project situation and the surrounding issues. When you get to this point in your presentation, it is a good idea to stop and ask if anything has changed about the project. You want to be sure that you are focused on the right things before proceeding. It might be good to have a couple of alternatives in mind just in case they voice a wish for additional or different information.

Point out how the client benefits from using your team's approach. In the body, you'll use examples, testimonials, and project write-ups to clarify and prove your point. Keep every piece of information relevant.

- Make your transitions smooth. Stay focused on what you want them to remember.
- Your final comments should be centered on the call to action. You might say, "We can be on the job as soon as a decision is made."

Make an Impression. The first five minutes—the introduction—is your only chance to make a first impression. You can show the client you are enthusiastic and excited about the project, and lay out compelling reasons why your team is the right choice. You must quickly set the tone of your information—stand out. Otherwise, the listeners will feel that you are nothing more than one more face in the crowd of presenters they'll be seeing stream through their conference room in the next few hours.

Be bold, authoritative, and confident without arrogance. What you say shapes the rest of the presentation. If you make bold statements such as, "Our job during this next thirty minutes is hard; we're going to have to get you to agree to change the way you do things," the listeners will sit up and take notice. If you are tentative and say something like, "We *believe* we are well-suited to conduct this work," listeners will fall into complacency. Hold their attention by being passionate about what you are presenting.

You will want to speak in "technicalese." As a technical professional, it's your comfort zone. It's easy for you to lapse into a nuts-and-bolts discussion. The panel, however, doesn't want to hear it, at least not as much as you do. Avoid too much detail of the technical elements about the project itself. As a general rule, the decision-makers are more interested in the outcome, the benefits, and in the team that will be involved in making it all happen. Keep in mind that it is very likely some of the decision-makers will *not* be a technical person, which is why it is best to talk more about the client and their issues and concerns, rather than about the technical details of how a project will be managed.

Stay Focused on Client Needs. Be sure to have a complete understanding of the project and the client's specific issues and needs. This is the time to remember that it's not just about your people but what your people can do for the client—that's the selling point. A good rule of thumb is for your presentation to be 60 percent about the client and 40 percent about your company strengths to meet the client's needs.

Talk about the client needs, the project, innovative ideas and techniques you will employ to solve the client's problems, and the benefits. The winning presentation will be the one that has solid specific content that reflects the client's true needs. If it is not specific, then it is just another dog-and-pony show.

Make a Seating Chart. As people arrive, make a quick seating chart so that you can use their names as you speak. It also helps later when you are recalling a comment that someone on the selection committee made. You can just look at your chart and be reminded of who made the statement.

Who is the Decision-Maker? Do you know how to spot the final decision-maker in a group? Even though they are technically supposed to make this decision as a group, there is usually an individual that carries more weight on the decision. If you will notice, it is usually the person that everyone gives deference to, or who everyone looks to when you ask if there are any questions. You still need to be careful to make eye contact and to address all the members with your comments.

Introductions. Before you get into the content of the presentation, give the committee a basic orientation of who's who and how they fit into the overall organization chart for the project. Present this information from the perspective of how it benefits the client.

You might say something like, "This is Joe, he is an expert in (Joe's area) and here's what it means to you..." instead of just introducing Joe by name. This is the time to establish the credibility of the individuals that will be involved in the project. Know the decision-making team's hot buttons and tie the introductions to them. Help the decision-maker recognize why he or she needs your team to provide solutions, and then motivate him or her to desire them. Introduce each other, but then return the focus of the conversation back to the selection committee.

The Team. In your short-list presentation you must show how dynamic, communicative, and committed your team is—what is the best way to do that?

For some firms, this portrayal of *team* is easy. A firm with a low turnover rate may be able to propose a team with a proven track record of successful project experience together for many years. But often, the interview presentation teams will be composed of disparate professionals. Perhaps you have strategically included sub-consultants on the team. Maybe it is a joint venture. Maybe you have created a brand-new team from internal staff based on their particular areas of expertise, but with little to no experience of actually working *together*. How in the world can that team come across as compatible, innovative, and easy to work with?

The client wants assurance that the team can work together without disruption to their project. Team delivery can be challenging because of how individuals speak, how transitions are made between speakers, and how groups of team members move around the space. Memorable presentations are well choreographed without being overly staged. When team members are so comfortable with each other that they have fun and support one another throughout all stages of the presentation, it becomes more meaningful and memorable to the client. This generally happens when the group rehearses until it becomes second nature to them.

Clients typically want to see the proposed project manager doing most of the talking. However, it is usually best to begin the presentation with your strongest and best presenter; it creates a positive perception and sets the dynamics for the entire group. As you begin speaking, keep in mind that you'll have about thirty seconds to catch and focus their attention.

Start right off with something that is of interest to them. Know what they want to hear and use it as a hook to catch their attention. Don't just start with, "I'm so-and-so and I'm very happy to be here."

For instance, if you are talking about building a football stadium, you probably have the coach there as part of the selection committee. Say something about how important football is to the university: "Football—it requires individual effort and great teamwork. We want to show you how our company will provide top-notch individual effort and coordinated teamwork to give you the project you want."

By presenting your information in this way, you've started off on a positive note of excitement that shows you understand how important this project is to them. Show your personality, and show that you are caught up in the excitement of working with them. Sound committed and excited about this project, and connect with the owners that value it.

Make your presentation strong and powerful by starting with a visual structure or diagram. It helps you cover all the material in an organized way and leaves the impression that you care enough to be prepared. It will also help to transition from one topic to another.

Use the general approach of:

- Tell them what you're going to tell them.
- Tell them your purpose statement or selling point.
- In your wrap-up, tell them again what you just told them.

The End. Finishing strong is very important because sometimes the beginning and the end will be all they remember! Bring them back to the key points of your presentation. It's OK if you repeat. Most adults will forget 90 percent of what you told them within an hour of hearing it unless there is a compelling reason to remember. A good trick is to tell them that you *want* them to remember. Say, "I want you to remember this…" and then repeat it. There is just something about hearing the words instructing them to do so that helps people to remember points. Return to your key point often during the presentation and end with a call to action: "We are ready to begin as soon as we receive a call from you to proceed!"

Watch Your Time. Allow enough time for each element of the presentation. If you are using a PowerPoint presentation, you can generally estimate about two minutes per slide. During the presentation, have someone sit behind the audience and signal you when your piece of the presentation time is almost up, and then signal again when it is time to shut up and sit down. It's very important that you do not go over your time allowance. Plan well so that you never go past your time limit. Presenters going over the allowed time may receive immediate negative points. It may be perceived as lack of planning and management skills.

If an hour is allowed for the presentation, the time schedule might look something like this:

1. Tell what you're going to talk about in the first five minutes—make your selling point.
2. Tell why they should choose your firm in the next five minutes.
3. Tell what they want to hear about how you will manage their project in the next ten minutes.
4. Ask for questions in the remaining twenty to thirty minutes.
5. End by telling them again what you told them in the last five minutes, again pointing out your selling points.

The impact of communication is more about how words are delivered than it is about the words themselves. It's the chemistry, personality, body language, and eye contact. Short-list presentations are a group of people communicating with another group of people. It is important to be personable and connect with the individuals. Ultimately this decision will be an emotional decision.

As mentioned previously, the human brain typically processes communication as:

- 7 percent being the words we use
- 35 percent from the sound of the voice—whether it is confident, strong, and comfortable

- 55 percent is nonverbal. The nonverbal aspects are transmitted through our appearance, posture, the gestures we make, eye contact, and the facial expressions we make while speaking.

Face your audience—don't talk to the slides. It is best to talk in a normal tone of voice, just as you would at the office. Remember to always keep your shoulders squared to the audience, and make eye contact with individuals. Study the next chapter on presentation skills and practice many times. Good presentation skills will help to win a higher percentage of projects and increase revenue for the company.

It's Not About You. All eyes are on you, and most people would be nervous. The reason everyone's eyes are on you is not to judge you, but because they want to hear your answer to their question, "What can you do for me?" Whoever does that better in their short-list presentation wins the contract.

Visuals are less important than the need to keep the presentation personal. Plan them last, after the presentation is developed. Make sure your visuals complement your theme and do not take over the presentation. The selection committee is primarily interested in getting to know the people on the team that they will be working with on this project. Some people say you should not even use PowerPoint for these presentations and that it is more effective to use flip charts and boards to accentuate your points. Some feel that PowerPoint becomes the object of the presentation rather than the information. Also some tend to rely on it as crutch instead of talking to the individuals present. It is your choice for what works best for your presentation and what feels most comfortable to you.

Whatever you decide, plan the visuals only after the content is established. Visuals must match the strategy and have a clear reason to be included. Scale them large enough for people to see from the back of the room without straining.

Handouts. Save the details of the presentation for a handout that you give the selection committee at the end of your presentation. The reason you give it to them at the end is so that they will not be tempted to read it instead of listening to you.

Speakers. Generally the selection committee wants to hear from the project manager and those that will be working on the project. Choose your primary speakers wisely and work with them until they are confident and at ease. The initial introduction and summary comments can be made by the best speaker in the group, leaving the audience with a positive impression.

Dress the Part. Appearance is very important, especially when making presentations; it creates an unspoken message and a perception of credibility. Keep in mind that this short-list presentation is a performance—it is necessary to dress the part that you are going to play. When in doubt, it's always safe to dress one notch above your audience. They want you to look like the professional that they are going to pay to do this project for them.

Do whatever you need to do to look like a professional who warrants what you will be charging the client for this project. Consider wearing your glasses if you normally wear them in order to look the part of a professional. Men should consider wearing a suit and tie. You can always remove the jacket once you get there if it is seems to be too much. Women should wear a skirt or a nice pantsuit. Be careful to avoid distractions with your appearance, such as a short skirt, cleavage, too much jewelry or makeup, or very high heels. Shoes should be clean and scuff free. Do whatever you need to do to look the part of the highly paid technical professional.

Appear Organized. Perception is reality and we begin judging people the instant we see them. If you begin your presentation by looking all flustered and disorganized, the audience will assume that there is a question about your credibility and your capabilities to handle this project.

When it is your turn to speak:

1. Look organized by standing tall and moving purposefully.
2. Walk up from a standing position from the back or side of the room if possible. You will have better blood circulation when you have been standing, you can think more clearly, and you will be less prone to feel nervous if you're already standing when you start.
3. Set your notes down and establish eye contact with a few people nearby.
4. Pause for three or four seconds; it captures their attention.
5. Smile—you look great!
6. Clearly state your purpose and launch into your presentation with confidence.
7. Be passionate and excited about this project!

Rehearsal. It is very important to rehearse your presentation as a team. Go over it at least three times. This helps you to know how long each person's piece of the presentation will take and how best to transition to the next speaker. Rehearse a mock question-and-answer (Q&A) session using questions that you might expect to receive. A good way to practice the Q&A is to write down every possible question on 3 x 5 cards, shuffle them, and then practice answering each question as if hearing it for the first time. A number of possible questions are included at the end of this chapter.

Questions. Most short-list presentations will give you an allotted time for telling your story, and then they want to ask questions of you. Welcome this opportunity; it can be the most significant time of your presentation if managed properly. This is a good time to share material that you did not have time to cover in your presentation. Keep your answers simple and to the point, returning often to your selling points as much as possible. Use the person's name when addressing him or her with your answer.

Determine ahead of time who will answer specific questions. However, keep in mind that the more people speaking, the more time will be used from your allotted time. During the Q&A session, do not correct or compensate for each other's shortcomings unless it is very critical. Doing so will cause the entire team to lose credibility. If correction is necessary, try to address it later when it's your turn to speak, and do so without focusing on the individual.

Maintain a moving-forward attitude during the Q&A session by moving toward the person asking, and welcome each question. It makes the individual feel a part of the offered solution.

During the Q&A session, be aware of your expressions and maintain strong body language. Stay calm and remember to square your shoulders to the person you are addressing. Avoid glancing elsewhere in the room while a question is being asked. Continue to maintain eye contact and focus on the person speaking. Having the ability to do this shows your confidence. If you're unsure of where the person is coming from with this question, watch the body language to determine if this question is coming from a hostile or defensive position. Lock on to the questioner and concentrate on the question and the underlying needed information. Take your time in formulating your response.

If you get a multi-part question, just break it down into parts. You can say something such as, "The first part of your question has to do with…"

and then answer that part. Next say, "The second part of Joe's question was…" and move on to the next part. You can also buy yourself time to think by rephrasing the question or by saying, "Let me make sure I understand your question." When you have completed your answer, turn to the person who asked it to confirm that your response answers the question.

Neutralize negative questions by rephrasing them. A questions such as, "Why are your fees so much higher?" can be rephrased as, "Your question has to do with how we structure our fees."

Pause often. Pausing to gather your thoughts can be very powerful. It shows that you value the question and want to give it the best response. With your answers, try to bring the focus back to the selling points of your presentation in order to tie it all together. Decide who will be responsible for answering each type of question and rehearse it a few times.

Be alert for questions that you are not qualified to answer, such as legal or tax questions. On any subject, it is OK to refer to another person in the group who might be more qualified to answer. Maintain your composure when you get questions that you did not expect. If you don't know the answer, don't bluff as you will lose credibility. Offer to find the answer and get back by a certain date, and then be sure to call them back.

The Close. Make the close brief and memorable. Close with an energetic finish that shows excitement about this project and working for this client. During your last five minutes, review the strategic selling points and *ask* for the job. Using our earlier example about the football stadium, you could say something such as this: "Our team wants to work with you to ensure that you get the facility that reflects both the proud heritage of the university and this university's winning future!" It may sound silly to you, but it will be music to their ears!

Remember, a winning short-list presentation is a group of people connecting with another group of people. The groups are the project team members communicating with the client to convince the selection committee that you are best qualified to address the issues and concerns for this project. You are communicating that you can do it better than the competition, and that the people in your firm are the best choice for this project. You will create that perception through the strategy, style and structure of how you give your short-list presentation.

The short-list presentation is not about you, or how nervous you are. It is about getting a message, or story, across to the client that addresses their issues and concerns. You are going to do it much better than your competition will.

The decision will be based on whom the client feels they would be most comfortable working with each day on this project. All the firms are qualified, or they would not be presenting. In the end, the winner will be the one that the client has a good feeling about and that the committee thinks is different and better than all the rest. Ultimately, the short-list interview is a personal and emotional decision based on how well the team is liked and respected by the selection committee.

Key Concepts in this Chapter

1. Planning for the short list presentation begins as soon as the proposal is out the door.
2. The reason for a shortlist interview is so that the project owner can meet the people who will be involved in the project.
3. Structure the message to show how each individual will address client issues and concerns.
4. Don't say the same things as in the proposal.
5. Rehearse at least 3 times as a group.

6. Make sure the main presenter has good presentation skills.
7. Prepare and practice some of the questions that might be asked of you and decide who will answer each type of question.

Welcome questions from the selection committee, but be prepared. Choose possible questions from the following list that might be appropriate for the type of work your firm will do, and have the team rehearse answering them.

Potential Questions to Rehearse for the Short-List Presentation

1. How do you handle project oversight and observation? Is it managed in-house or do you use an outside firm?
2. What is your communication process? How will we communicate?
3. What tools or systems will be used to monitor quality and schedule?
4. When project budget isn't adequate, at what point do you bring this problem to us?
5. How will the company principal's be involved?
6. How do you treat and control costs?
7. What methods will you use to monitor the schedule?
8. How does the project manager control, report, and monitor activities of the team?
9. Have you used or do you have experience with our required system?
10. Can your firm supply us with a copy of your most recent annual financial report?
11. How is work coordinated in your office?
12. What does your existing workload look like? How will this job fit it?
13. How will you manage your present workload in addition to our project?
14. What other project has the project manager done that is comparable in size to this project?
15. What is the largest job your firm has done?

16. What is your average billing volume?
17. How do you handle scope changes as they relate to schedule and cost impact?
18. What is your quality review process? Who will do quality review?
19. Who leads the engineers?
20. Have you completed a schedule for this job? How will you manage it?

If TEAMING with another firm

1. Which joint project between your two firms is most relevant to the proposed project?
2. How do you expect to handle the fact that you have never worked together on any other project?
3. Do you have a contractual arrangement? What is it?
4. How can we be sure your firms will be compatible?
5. How will you distribute responsibility?
6. Which members of this team have worked on which jobs?
7. What communications method will be used between the two of you?
8. Where is the proposed project office?
9. How will other offices integrate with local office?
10. When the team is geographically separated: How do you expect to coordinate?
11. How do you expect this team to work together if you've never done so before?

STAFFING

1. If additional personnel were required to accelerate the project's progress, what would be their capability from within your firm? Will they be available?
2. If you should get a bigger job than ours, will your people be pulled away?

3. What rate of personnel turnover do you have?

4. Can you guarantee that we will get those present here on our project?

5. Is all of the team you've designated for this project out of the same office? If not, how will that work?

6. If we give you a start date, how would that affect the staffing projections?

7. How many people will be in the project office? How will it be staffed?

8. Will your sub-consultants be in the project office?

9. As a project manager, will you be involved in other projects besides ours?

10. Does your project manager do all of this type work for the company? If so, how can he or she handle all of that in addition to our project?

11. Who is the single direct contact for us?

12. Are the support team members assigned to perform field visits during construction?

13. Give us examples of field personnel qualifications.

14. Is the project manager really going to be the one doing the work?

15. As project manager, what jobs are you working on currently? Will they interfere with working on ours?

16. As project manager, what do you feel you've learned from other jobs that can be applied to ours?

17. Does the project manager really understand the intensity of our schedule and the concerns surrounding this project?

18. How many technical staff and individual disciplines are represented? Do you understand you are an extension of our staff?

19. What percent of your time do you, as an individual, expect to spend on this job? (The question may be addressed to each person.)

20. What is the largest related project that you as an individual have worked on?

21. Has anyone in your firm ever worked at the site? On a similar project?

COSTS and PROJECT EXPERIENCE

1. Why are your fees so high?
2. Who will we be negotiating with on this contract?
3. Is this budget sufficient for this job?
4. Has your range of bids for subcontractors been tight? How many bidders have you had?
5. Please describe your firm's experience and technical competence in comparable work.
6. Describe your firm's current and projected workload during the planned period of performance.
7. Expand on past experience your firm has had working with the other firms listed in your proposal.
8. Size-wise, how does this project fit into your overall workload history?
9. What percentage of change orders on the project you are describing was your fault?
10. What litigation have you had as a result of errors or omissions?
11. How was administration handled on project X (a project you might have shown in your proposal)?
12. How does your Project Manager coordinate work? (This would be a good flowchart visual.)
13. Do your engineers do cost estimating? How detailed would your cost estimates be after preliminaries?
14. Describe your field inspection capabilities.
15. Describe each project history and the people who worked on each one. (Go to a people matrix if you have one.)
16. What is your most recently completed similar job?
17. What is your awareness of regulatory standards?
18. Be aware that a series of energy conservation questions may be asked.

19. What factors do you feel are important to this job? (These may include design issues, site, traffic, utilities, access, and so forth.)

20. How many years has the company been in business? Doing what?

21. Be prepared to answer specific questions about project write-ups.

22. What form of specifications do you use? Do you have a department that works on specs? How does that work? Can you do nonproprietary-type specs?

23. Who does the XYZ task? (This same question may be asked for any of the specifics named in the RFP.)

13

SPEAKING AND PRESENTATIONS

As part of your Business Development efforts, you will find many opportunities to give presentations to groups of people. You may be called upon to present your company's capabilities, give a technical white paper, or participate in a short-list interview. Embrace the opportunity and be confident about your speaking ability.

Anyone can be a good public speaker with a little practice—actually, everyone is a public speaker. Every time you speak within earshot of another human, your speech and body language will make an impression. Even when you listen, you're making an impression. Your body language is projecting a message to the person talking to you, even if you don't utter a word!

Becoming a good speaker is a learned skill. Just as with any other skill, if you want to be good at giving presentations, you must commit to learning and improving your abilities. It helps to study others that do it well. Practice a lot and seek objective feedback.

The ability to present well gives you a competitive advantage in business, and has many benefits for the company as well as for the individual. You gain credibility for both yourself and your company. Speaking skillfully creates for you the image of a person of authority and a strong leader. Acquiring good oral communication skills will allow you to excel at inspiring and motivating other people.

As you speak, it is important to appear confident and in control, but to also show your personality and passion for the subject. Passionate people are just more persuasive and interesting. The perception of confidence and passion can be accomplished through nonverbal messages, including body language. The easiest ways to accomplish this is to stand tall while speaking, and to know what you are talking about.

Use your hands to gesture for emphasis, but then return them naturally to your side. The base position for your hands is always relaxed and at your side unless gesturing. You appear more open, relaxed, confident, and in charge when your hands are still.

Don't Hold Anything. If you use a pointer or eraser while giving your talk, put it back down after use. Holding something just encourages nervous clicking, twisting, or fidgeting—a sign of weakness. There is seldom a reason for the hands to touch each other except to make a particular point. It makes you appear nervous and is distracting to the audience.

- When the hands go together, everyone looks to see what is in them. So just keep them loosely and comfortably at your sides. Or, if you are seated, keep them resting on the tabletop or in your lap.
- Be in control of your body position, but not stiff—you want to give the impression that you are calm and comfortable.
- Feel free to move, but never pace back and forth.
- Step forward to make a point. Walk over to an individual and make eye contact to emphasize something or to listen to his or her question.

The average adult attention span is only fifteen to thirty seconds, so if you mess up they're not going to remember as long as your message is clear and directed at their needs. Focusing the spotlight on the audience helps you to direct your energy on to them. It's not about you; the presentation is about them and the message. You have information of interest to present, and you only have a few minutes to accomplish that task so you want to make the most of it.

Don't Apologize. Never tell them you were not prepared to speak, or apologize, or make statements such as, "I'm not good at speaking in front of people." They don't want to hear that. They want you to do well and they're on your side! Don't apologize for anything; just do the best you can and the audience will appreciate your effort.

Rehearse, Rehearse. It's normal to be apprehensive about speaking in front of people. The best way to overcome fear of speaking is to rehearse many times. Remember, you know more about your subject than they do, so just relax. When you practice, do so in three to five minute increments. It makes it easier to remember more of what you want to say. Another way to prepare is to memorize the first few phrases of each section—not word for word, but enough so that they come easily and naturally. It's OK to use a cheat sheet with your key points available so that you can glance at it when needed.

Never read your speech, except for the times that might require reading parts as the purpose of your talk. That could be a book reading, a legal document, or something that must be presented word for word such as a quote or reference article.

Before you arrive to give your presentation, take a few minutes to calm yourself and visualize your success. Practice some deep breathing to refresh your oxygen. Take a walk, or get a little exercise beforehand.

As you begin your presentation, relax, be yourself, and try to enjoy the process of addressing the needs and concerns of the audience with the information you have to give. Remember that people are people—just like you. They want you to do well.

Arrive Early. Arrive an hour before you are scheduled to begin your presentation to check the room layout and equipment. If this is a short-list presentation, spend thirty minutes preparing the room so that your team is the center of focus in front of the decision-makers. Arrange the room so that your decision-maker or audience is facing away from any windows or distractions. You have only a few minutes of their attention and you want all of it. Make sure the equipment is working properly, and set up your visual aids (boards, charts, etc.). Save handouts until the end unless the audience needs them for reference during your presentation. If they have them in hand, they will read them instead of listening to you.

Own the Room. As people begin to arrive, mingle and learn their names. You'll feel more comfortable and will be able to relate on a personal level if you can recall a few names. You should appear to own the room. You are responsible for the success or failure of this session, so make it work for you. Turn your attention to the individuals as they enter the room. If this is a client meeting, find out whom they are and learn their areas of responsibility. You might want to make a seating chart to inconspicuously refer back to during your talk. People will be impressed when you use their names during the presentation.

Introduce Yourself as People Arrive. You will be introducing yourself and shaking hands with people as they enter the room, and during any networking time. Make sure you have a good handshake, as this is their first interaction with you.

Relate to the Individual. Once you get the floor, remember to relate to the individuals in the audience. Square your shoulders and *face a person*—never look at the floor, ceiling, or the screen while talking. Focus on one person at a time. As you speak, focus on one person for five seconds—or until you complete a point—and then move on to another person. This one takes a little practice.

Making eye contact is important, but don't stare; overdoing it can cause the other person to feel uncomfortable. Try to maintain a natural connection, which will work best if you don't think about it too much because then it becomes artificial.

When Writing on a Board. If you're writing on a board or easel, say what you are going to write—then turn and write it. Turn back to your audience to talk about what you just wrote. It's OK to glance at the board for an outline or notes occasionally and then back at the audience to speak.

Be Mindful of Body Language. Use meaningful body language and gestures when giving your talk. Some interesting things happen with body language. You can create an instant perception or change the meaning of the words coming from your mouth with the message your body gives. Make sure your body language and your words match in business and in your personal life. If they do not match, then your message is confusing.

Understanding body language is a good way to make sure you are presenting the message you want to give, and how your message is being read by the audience. For example:

- Hands in pockets may be interpreted to mean nonchalant, passive, or overconfident—exhibiting a lack of concern.
- Keep your hands comfortable at your sides unless using them for gesturing.

- Fig leaf (hands clasped in front) makes you appear timid, inexperienced, and vulnerable. You often see this in photos when people are not sure what to do with their hands.
- Arms crossed while leaning back in the chair or facing away from you could mean that the individual is feeling restrained and closed off, does not believe your message, or is not receiving the information.
- Hands-on-the-hips posture is perceived as defiant or challenging.
- Hands behind the back could mean that something is hidden. Your audience will unconsciously be curious and distracted about what's back there.

Present From a Standing Position. It's always best to present from a standing position when possible. It allows you to move for emphasis, and to stand tall and natural, with hands at your side. You will appear more confident, persuasive, and knowledgeable about what you are talking about. You will also have better breathing for a stronger voice. Presenting from a standing position just creates a more dynamic atmosphere.

Don't Pace. It is good to move, especially if addressing a large audience, but avoid pacing. Pacing too much gives the impression of nervousness. Address one side of the room and then another. Stay in position until your point is complete before moving.

From a Seated Position. When you must speak from a seated position, try to position yourself at the table so that you are the focal point. Be sure to turn toward the person you are speaking to and make eye contact each time you speak. Your forearms may be resting comfortably on the table and hands should be about eight inches in from the edge of the table when gesturing. This position comes across as confident and powerful. No elbows on the table, and never rest your head on your hands or else you will look bored.

Strive to be natural, but don't fidget. When it is your turn to listen, relax with your hands in your lap. Keep your hands separated so that you don't inadvertently start wringing your hands or doing something that makes you look nervous. Avoid touching the face, which is usually interpreted as a sign of dishonesty or uncertainty. It can also come across as a feminine characteristic.

If a group is making the presentation from a seated position, sit together on the same side of the table so that the client does not have to turn back and forth between speakers as if watching a ping-pong ball or a tennis match.

Podium. Try to avoid standing behind a podium if at all possible. A podium cuts you off from the audience. Walk up and place your notes there, but move around to the side or in front of it—don't lean on it.

There may be situations that force you to speak from behind a podium, such as when you are speaking to a large audience and the only microphone is attached to the podium. There are ways you can make the best of the situation. Place your notes toward the back of the podium so that you can keep your head and eyes up. You can glance down at the notes without the audience seeing the top of your head.

Square your shoulders and speak to the group as if speaking to an individual. Be sure to make eye contact with all areas of the audience. Focus on first one side, the middle, and then the other side of the room. Remember the back of the room and make large sweeping gestures to include them.

Using Notes. If your subject is so complex that you need notes for reference, keep them as brief as possible. If your speech is long, a loose-leaf binder works well to hold notes and keep them in order. Once you are ready to speak, remove them from the binder so that you can slip each page to the side as you finish with it. Shuffling paper can be a distraction from your message. As you move the pages over, look up at your audience and continue with what you are saying, smoothly transitioning into the next page. They will never realize you went from one page to the next and are less likely to become distracted with wondering how many pages remain.

Gestures. Gestures help to deliver the message in a dynamic way, and the hands are a natural visual aid. By keeping the elbow slightly away from the ribcage, you can use your hands more freely and naturally. When speaking to a large audience, use large sweeping gestures, pointing with your entire hand to the back of the room in order to include them.

Be specific and defined when using hand gestures.

- For numbers, create a visual by holding up the corresponding number of fingers for such statements as "We have three (three fingers) objectives today," or "If you remember only one (one finger) thing…"
- Use opposing gestures to show comparisons such as an increase or decrease in numbers. With the table top or the other hand as a base, show relative distance between the two to emphasize your point. Dates or timelines can be shown by keeping one hand stationary and moving the other out from it to show the relative distance.
- For verbs that describe a situation, such as "growing," "expanding," or "eliminating"—demonstrate that changing motion with your hands. It may feel contrived to you, but your audience receives a visual statement that goes along with your words.
- When gesturing toward a visual such as a flip chart or exhibit board, gesture with the hand that is nearest to the visual, always keeping shoulders squared to the room and maintaining eye contact with your audience. Use the entire hand to indicate the chart like the weatherman—it's called the claw gesture.

Use each hand equally to gesture and then return them back to your sides. It may not feel natural to you for your hands to be at your sides but maintaining control of your hands makes you look more confident to the audience. Gesturing gives the audience a visual understanding of what you are trying to explain, but make sure your hands are not flailing about. Don't be in a rush; hold the gesture for two or three seconds, giving them plenty of time to grasp the concept. After emphasizing a point with a gesture, return your hands to their neutral position and arms comfortably (not stiff) at your side while speaking.

Voice. Your voice should show passion and interest in the subject, especially when you use words of strength. Project from the diaphragm to give your voice strength; people associate a strong voice with confidence. This does not mean loud. Use voice inflections and volume variations to maintain interest and to keep their attention. If your audience begins to show signs of boredom, ask a question or change your voice tone to bring them back.

Pause and change tempo at times to emphasize a point. The general pace should be to speak, pause, breathe, and speak. In this way, you are giving people time to take in the information. If you want to emphasize a particular point, say it, and then pause for a second in order to make a point of the importance of what you just said.

Eliminate Graffiti and filler words from your speech pattern. Avoid weak words such as, "I think." Filler words such as "um," "ahs," "you know," and "like, you know," may be fine for teenagers, but not for professionals. They do nothing to establish your credibility.

On the other hand, don't come across as condescending. Condescending words are those we add on to the end of sentences to make sure the audience understands. Used too often, they become annoying. Words such as "OK?" "See?" and "Right?" can leave the impression that the speaker is not sure that the audience is capable of grasping the meaning of what is being said.

Breathe. Remember to slow down and breathe. Deep breathing helps to relax the body. Breathing from the diaphragm will help to keep your voice strong. A strong—but not loud—voice will keep the audience's attention.

Be Careful What You Eat Before. Keep water within easy reach during your presentation in case you get a sudden scratchy throat. The day before and the day of your presentation, be careful what you eat and drink. You will be feeling a little nervous, so avoid caffeine—decaffeinated is OK.

Eat at least two hours prior to your presentation. You don't want to be hungry or your voice will be weak. On the other hand, if your stomach is too full, blood will be diverted to digestion and not to the brain where you need it in order to feel alert. Avoid foods or beverages that cause burping. As you speak, you inhale air, which could become a problem if you're feeling gassy already. Your mouth should be warm and moist, so stick to room-temperature water and avoid cold drinks. Some people find milk and citrus to be a problem so you might want to avoid them. Drink lots of water; eat fewer carbs and more protein. A high-protein diet seems to help with alertness and makes the voice stronger. Also, avoid those foods that are prone to cause bad breath such as onions, garlic, and spices.

Questions. If you take questions at the end of your presentation, make it memorable. Sometimes the only part of your presentation that will be remembered is the beginning and the end. When someone is asking you a question, move toward them, square your shoulders to them, and make eye contact. Watch the body language to get a clue about where the person is coming from with the question. Repeat the question in order to gain time to think of a good response. Repeating the question also helps to make sure the people in the back of the room hear, and to verify that you captured the question correctly. Show appreciation for the question, and form your answer so that it relates back to your topic. Address the room with your answer, but come back to the questioner to validate that you have answered the question. When time is up, let the audience know you can take only one more question. As a wrap-up, leave them with a strong memorable comment that ties your talk together.

Building the Presentation. There are a number of effective methods that can be used for presenting information to groups of people. Note cards work well if you know your subject well. Note cards can remind you of the highlights of what you want to say. This is the best way, because your talk will be more natural and you will connect with the audience more easily. Flip charts can work well for a small group, especially if the audience will be contributing information to the presentation.

If you plan to use a PowerPoint, keep these basics in mind:

- Never talk to the slides—talk to the audience.
- Locate the computer screen in front of you and just glance at it for reference.
- Don't read the slides; blend the bullet points naturally into your talk.
- Use dark background colors and light colors for the text.
- Keep text to a minimum and use a large easy-to-read font.
- Begin each line with a verb.
- Use no more than five to seven words per line.
- Use no more than five to seven lines per slide.
- Use color sparingly. Be aware that some people who are color blind may not see some combinations of colors, such as red and green, and brown and green.

Technical folks tend to get much too wordy on presentation slides. If you feel the need to explain a point in great detail, use handouts and distribute them just before the information is needed for reference.

Always bring a spare copy of your presentation in the event of technical difficulties. If you plan to distribute copies of the presentation, do so at the beginning so that your audience can make notes on them.

Make It Fun! Giving a presentation need not be that difficult when a few basics are mastered. Once you are into it, you may realize that you actually enjoy it. Above all, remember to be yourself. Don't try to be funny if it doesn't come easily for you, and never try to emulate a famous speaker just because you admire his or her style. Everyone has a different style, so be natural, be yourself, and show your personality. Presenting can be fun, so enjoy the experience. Know your material well and rehearse a lot, and you'll do great!

Key Concepts in this Chapter

1. The ability to present well gives you a competitive edge and technical professionals are often called upon to make public presentations.
2. Becoming a good public speaker is a learned skill that becomes easier with practice.
3. We discussed what to do with your hands and how to avoid distractions to your message.
4. Body language and voice patterns are important component of presenting information.
5. There are a number of effective methods of building visual support for presentations.

14

REFERRALS AND TESTIMONIALS

Simply doing good work is not enough—the people in a company must be able to *prove* that they do good work. The best way to do that is to let clients talk about how your firm measures up against your competition. The very best advertisement is always word-of-mouth recommendations or referrals. It costs you nothing, and there is a greater than 50 percent chance of winning the new work when a former client recommends your firm. Gaining a recommendation or referral from an existing client carries much more weight than if you say the same thing yourself. Referrals and testimonials can be the lifeblood for professional services companies.

Some firms tend to shy away from anything that appears to be sounding their own horn. To be successful in business, it must be done at every opportunity. If you can use your client's words to do it, the impact will be even greater.

So how do you get clients to recommend your firm to new prospects? And further, how can you get your networking contacts to refer your firm when they hear of an opportunity that would be a good fit? Start with gaining testimonials and recommendations from existing clients.

Testimonials from Existing Clients:

- **Quotes.** Use specific excerpts as quotes from any letters of appreciation they might have sent you. Just confirm with the authors that you may use them, and obtain their permission to pull the quote out of the full letter.

- **Capture even the most casual comments in writing.** You might say something like, "Thank you for that nice comment; it means a lot to me. May we use your statement in our marketing materials in order to attract more great clients like you?"

- **Ask for referrals while a project is in progress**. You can do this at various stages of the project as you ask if the client is satisfied. Let the client know you are proud of accomplishments to date and will continue the same level of service, then ask if they would be willing to provide an in-progress statement. You might consider writing the project progress to date in order to help get them started.

- **Show appreciation.** Any time a client gives you a recommendation or referral, always send a thoughtful handwritten thank-you note. An e-mail will do, but a true piece of mail is so rare these days that just the fact you made this effort will go a long way toward increasing your stature in the eyes of the client.

- **Make it easy.** Clients are busy and preoccupied. Make it easy for them to articulate their thoughts of appreciation about the work you've done. Out of respect for their time, and rather than asking clients to face a blank page, offer to provide a template letter to which changes or additions can be made. You might also offer thought-provoking questions to get them started such as:

  o What were your main concerns before we started working for you?

  o How are our people to work with?

  o What did you discover when we started working together?

 o What value did we bring to the project?

 o Why would you think other firms would benefit from working with us?

Encourage Staff. Help your staff to understand the importance of obtaining references and testimonials. Encourage them to listen for opportunities to capture positive words from clients. During staff meetings, help them to recall comments and feedback they might have received from clients and expand those into testimonials. Give them some phrases to use to gather additional comments from existing clients such as:

- "I am glad you are pleased with our work; would it be all right if my company used your comments in our marketing materials?"
- "I really appreciate your kind words; may I paraphrase your comments into a testimonial so that we may attract other clients like you? I will let you review and approve the finished document first, of course."
- "Thank you for your nice e-mail. Can you expand your comments further on why our work is of value to you? May I have your permission to use your comments in our marketing materials?"

Keep in mind that there are many scenarios for obtaining recommendations or testimonial comments. Some situations will be as simple as receiving a complimentary e-mail or a comment in a conversation. Other times it may be the rescue of an on-the-edge project that went south but was retrieved thanks to your firm's excellent guidance.

Referrals from Your Personal Network. Show peers and others how they can help you. Make it easy for them to be good referral sources and to help make connections for you. It is your responsibility to educate them as to how they can best help—maybe it is intelligence gathering or a phone or e-mail introduction to a target client. Try to be as specific as possible with the information you need and the type of clients and projects that would benefit your firm. Be specific about what your ideal client looks like: core competencies, size, and industry sector. The more specific you can be, the more likely you are to spark ideas about how they can help you. Always acknowledge and show appreciation for the efforts that are made on your behalf.

Be a Good Referral Source Yourself. Make an effort to frequently help others connections with their target clients. Watch for opportunities to put people together that could work together. You will be viewed as a valuable resource by both parties.

Think of It as a Checking Account. Help others and they will help you. Gaining referrals within your personal network works a lot like a bank checking account. You must periodically make deposits in order to expect to be able to make withdrawals. It's unrealistic to expect others to refer your firm if you are not doing your part to be an active referral source for them. For you to be able to refer and help others, you will need to ask questions about their needs and target clients and listen for ways that you might help them. Your efforts will eventually come back to you.

If you are not comfortable endorsing another firm without having had firsthand experience, you can simply make introductions and then let them handle it from there. An introduction is a great gift, but an endorsement must be earned.

To sustain and grow your business, testimonials and referrals are essential. Help others first. Do everything you can to be a good referral source and connector. Make it easy for others to do the same for you by letting them know how they can help you.

Key Concepts in this Chapter

1. Because selling professional service is abstract, testimonials from satisfied clients is crucial to gaining new work.
2. Word of mouth is the least costly and most effective method for advertising your services.
3. Testimonials can come from existing clients, past clients, and personal networks.
4. Encourage staff to ask for referrals and testimonials as part of each project.
5. Be a good referral source for others.

Key Concepts in this Chapter

1. Because selling professional service is abstract, testimonials from satisfied clients is crucial to winning new work.
2. Word of mouth is the least costly and most effective method for advertising your services.
3. Testimonials can come from existing clients, past clients, and personal networks.
4. Encourage staff to ask for referrals and testimonials at the end of each project.
5. Be a good referral source for others.

15

INTERNET-BASED MARKETING

Most professional services firms will benefit from some kind of an online presence. The Internet can help people find you and gather information about your business. It provides a way for them to determine if they can use your services.

Internet-based marketing should be a complement to the personal one-on-one connections that lead to long-term relationships and help you to grow your business. For a small company, an online presence can be as simple as a website that lists your services, or it can be as complex as you have the time and money to spend on it.

Don't get caught up in the technology, as it is expanding and changing at an astoundingly rapid pace and can be a distraction as well as over-whelming and intimidating. You would need to spend hours each day just to stay current with new advances. Measure the amount of time you have available for such activity. It's easy to spend many hours working on building the perfect website and working on social media and writing blogs can become addictive. Depending on the type of service you offer, focusing on one or two media options, and doing them well, will be the most effective approach.

Many of the best and most effective Business Development tools are simple and are not costly. Analyze the return on the time spent on Internet-based marketing. While it may help you to feel that you are doing Business Development, online activities alone are not enough for the professional services firm. Recent research shows that the way people *find* your business may be changing, but people still buy from people they know and trust. That will always remain true for professional services firms. It still takes both personal interactions as well as an online presence to make it work.

Website. Compared to print advertising, online marketing is relatively inexpensive. It works for you constantly and is easy to track and measure. As the owner of a small company, you will become distracted from marketing activities with billable work, and may not have time for networking and outside marketing activities as often as you would like. The website continues to work for you. Just remember to follow up on leads as soon as possible in order to capture the opportunity. Your website can also provide support for those Business Development folks out making face-to-face contacts.

The website is the window to your business. It is a method of *pull* lead generation. It explains who you are and what you do and will pull traffic to your site by using SEO (Search Engine Optimization) words. This is the way Google and other search engines will rank your site when a potential client enters words that are relevant to their particular problem. You must know what those terms are and monitor your website for ways to include them. Obtain the services of a professional designer that is up on the latest SEO tools.

More and more time-strapped people, especially younger professionals, are using their computers as a means of locating solutions to their problems. Your website must be designed to generate leads and reflect the professional capabilities of the firm. The trick here is that you must follow up immediately when you get a website-generated lead. Otherwise, the prospect will call another company who is more responsive, and you've lost out.

Assign Online Media Responsibility. If you decide to make your online presence one of the lead-generation tools for the company, assign someone full time whose primary focus is the online world. To be done correctly it requires consistency and attention. Nothing is worse than incomplete or outdated information. This person's responsibility will be to gather information from the technical team and write blogs and other website materials, and to keep the website current and updated.

The Internet marketing coordinator will capture and respond to registration information when people visit the site, and send out e-mail newsletters and other promotional information. This individual can also keep social media sites current and can post on and monitor sites such as LinkedIn, Facebook, and Twitter if you decide to use them. He or she might also place educational videos on YouTube and other sites that your industry finds valuable. If an online presence is to be an effective lead-generation tool, it requires an enormous amount of attention and an investment of time and money. The world of on-line social media is growing and changing rapidly and requires a dedicated focus to make it valuable to the professional service firm.

Develop a Following. Bringing people back to your website repeatedly will help to keep your firm top of mind when they need your service. Here are several ways to keep them coming back.

- Provide technical and current information that is of interest. Include links back to your website and to other sites for support information.

- Give them something that is entertaining, such as music. Just make sure it fits with the image that you want to maintain.

- Make them smile or even laugh. Is it possible that your name or one of your services can be humorous? Even if your branding is not funny, you can still (tastefully) poke fun at yourself, or the industry, or an event. Hold a contest for the funniest joke or picture. Spell out the rules and have someone monitor entries for appropriateness before they go live.

- Offer creativity on your website. If your firm provides a service that can have a creative influence, find ways to build in an interactive application that keeps bringing people back.

Your site will develop a following as you build trust through useful, practical educational content that is not self-promoting. Those in your target market will come to recognize and rely on the information you have posted, and will return often for additional information. They will think of you first when they have a need.

Face-to-Face Interaction is Still Required. As much as some would have you believe that all that is necessary to promote your business is to have the perfect website or other online marketing tool—it just isn't so. The more professional your service offerings, that more the need will be to interact with people face-to-face. Would you plan surgery or other complex professional service online, and let that be the only deciding factor as to which doctor will do your surgery? Of course not! You might locate a surgeon online and check his or her credentials, but you want to know and trust a human before proceeding. It's the same with any other truly professional service. Online is a great way for a prospect to find you (as well as your competitors), but you still need to have people skills, and interact with people often, in order to build your business.

Clear Message. Professional services branding is driven by expertise and client relationships. Your website must state clearly what you do and how your firm is different. Your online message must be clear and concise and specifically written for your targeted audience. You can post a great deal of backup information such as projects and resumes, but the initial message should be simple and straightforward.

A clear compelling message is the reason that potential clients will come to you before they call your competitors. The problem for some is that this message is extremely difficult to craft and to get right.

It's important to know and understand how your clients feel about your company and the work that you do. Your message must be about what is important to your clients, and it must be different from all the rest. Write content from the client's perspective. How does it benefit them? If you are saying the same thing as most other firms, your message will fall on deaf ears. The client must perceive that your firm is different in the areas that are important to them, and all of your materials must back up that message.

Consistent branding for your company is important. Studies prove that the company with a strong, easy-to-understand, believable differentiator will be three times more likely to grow. Don't be afraid of losing business by having an exclusive clear message. When you can show specialization, your odds of winning work increase substantially—especially when it comes to online marketing. You will actually generate more business by having a defined and clear focus. Ask your clients what is of most value to them. The more you can see yourself through the eyes of your preferred client, the easier it will be to develop a clear value-proposition message.

The Cost. Companies tend to worry too much about the costs of updating their websites. Building and managing a website, and the related costs, are coming down and becoming much more affordable. While the importance of face-to-face time with your potential clients will never be replaced, firms that embrace online marketing have a tremendous advantage. They will grow much faster and be more profitable. If you aren't keeping up with technology, you're falling behind in the industry. The majority of your competitors are investing in website updates. The cost to your business of doing nothing about your website far outweighs the amount of any investment that will be made.

New social media networking sites are springing up constantly. Use only sites that you can afford—both in time and money—to keep updated. You must choose those that make sense for your type of business. In this digital age, websites, blogs, and other online postings can be beneficial. Don't fear social media networking, but use cautiously and monitor often. Make sure the image being projected for your company is in keeping with your branding.

Keep content fresh, educational, interesting, and constantly changing. New postings need not take a lot of additional time. The content can come from information that was created for other purposes such as newsletter articles, proposals, project write-ups, and speeches. A single topic might be used for a speaking engagement, a website posting, a webinar, a blog, a social media posting, or as an article in your newsletter. You might want to identify a topic of the month and ask your technical professionals to contribute their perspectives. Pay attention to key words in the article that might pull prospective clients to your website for those looking for such information.

It's best to hire a professional to build and update your website, but you should educate yourself about SEO and the kind of content that draws your target prospects. Search engines reward high-quality and relevant content by directing more searches to your site, exposing your firm to new markets in all geographies and to potential clients that you might not even realize exist.

One of the beauties of online marketing is that it gives you the power to recognize what's working and what is not working. It gives you the ability to make adjustments to your marketing efforts immediately. Track the various marketing methods and determine which strategy works best for your business. Take the time to evaluate and review at least quarterly.

Evaluate to see if you are receiving the results you wanted and where you are receiving the best leads and the most activity. While data alone will not replace instinct and experience, having such knowledge will help you make well-informed decisions about where you should invest the greatest percentage of your marketing budget. Of course, networking and word-of-mouth advertising is always going to be the cheapest and best form of advertising for a professional services firm.

Social Media. There can be a place for social media in a professional services firm as long as it is monitored and controlled. You don't want everybody doing their own thing with the company name and information. Having a social media presence can help drive traffic to your website and is playing an increasing role in marketing professional services.

Many of these sites are also great places to track down a contact name at a target firm or to locate someone you've lost track of through the years. The challenge is to control the time spent on such sites as they can eat up an entire day very easily. Don't bite off too much, or you will drown in the possibilities. Make it fit your business, not the other way around.

Add social media buttons to your website to make it easy for people to follow your firm. It takes time to develop a following on social media, but it can have benefits. Depending on the types of services you offer, some of the benefits might be:

- **To Gain Company Visibility.** Maintaining a visible brand with repeat exposures can help to keep your firm top of mind when a client needs a service. You can regularly share information with existing and prospective clients on new regulations or other topics of interest. It provides the opportunity to position your expertise and highlight company expertise without coming across as selling it. Social media can provide the opportunity find leads for new business. It can also allow you to ask for referrals for new clients or for hiring new talent.

- **Individual Branding.** Technical professionals can demonstrate their areas of expertise on such sites as LinkedIn, YouTube, and Facebook. They can establish themselves as a resource and voice that people trust for a particular technical subject. Professionals can create the perception of being the expert, and are more likely to receive requests to speak at events and will be the person to call with questions about the topic.

- **Receiving Information.** You can quickly keep up with industry news or market changes and attitude shifts by keeping up with social media.

- **Find Partners.** By interacting with a number of people on a social media site, you may be able to find partnering situations, or the opportunity to share resources.

Direct Mail (e-mails). Modern direct mail marketing is driven by e-mail. Many people prefer e-mail to regular mail and know they can always opt out if they find it intrusive. Your e-mail lists can be one of your firm's greatest assets so it must be kept up-to-date, and the mailing must contain useful content in order to connect with your target audience. One way to build your e-mail list is to post valuable content behind a registration page on your website. Make sure this form is short and can be completed quickly, or some people will not take the time

Newsletters via e-mail and posted on your website can be very effective. Understand what your clients' interests are and how they will respond. Determine a consistent schedule so that they come to expect it and will watch for it.

Professional services firms will benefit most by implementing a mix of traditional marketing, such as networking and trade association activity, and the new online marketing options that are focused on content and social media. The more exposure you can have in both areas, the greater your increase of visibility and reputation within your target market.

<u>Key Concepts in this Chapter</u>

1. A website and an online presence can be valuable for most professional services firms when combined with face-to-face interactions.
2. There are many ways to draw potential clients to your website using the Internet.
3. The key to digital marketing is to have a clear and consistent message and know how your prospective clients search for information.
4. It is most effective for firms to have a person who is dedicated to maintaining blogs and social media accounts.

16

TIME MANAGEMENT

As a business owner of a professional services firm, your time is an important part of the product that you have to sell. The more efficient you can be with time, the more successful you will be in your business. By managing it closely you free up the time necessary for Business Development and other business building activities. Time must be viewed as a valuable resource that is to be managed wisely.

There are roughly 240 working and selling days in the year. When one is gone, there is no retrieving it. The best way to get a picture of where your time goes is to break the day into time slots for which you track the use of your time. Each day allots you only twenty-four hours so spend the majority of your time where it matters. You must learn to master the distractions that are causing loss of productivity by focusing on those things that are important to growing your business. Time cannot be managed unless you know where it goes.

Focus on results, not just activities. Will your activities make a difference at the end of the day? Time cannot be created or destroyed, but it can be maximized or wasted. An interruption may seem important at the time, but is it really a priority that is going to help you to reach your goal? Learning to correctly identify what is truly important can help you to focus on the work that needs to be done.

In order to use your time effectively, take the time to consider if a task is urgent or important. Successful people have learned to mentally categorize the tasks that need to be done each day. Does it require your time or could the task be delegated...or ignored?

Many people use a four quadrant matrix to categorize tasks into priorities. There are many variances but the basic concept is based on former president Eisenhower's time management method of placing each task into a quadrant of a box that defines the urgency and importance of it. Each item within the box can be further ranked using A, B, or C. Then it becomes clear which items should get tackled first, handled by someone else, or discarded. With practice the exercise of categorizing tasks becomes a mental habit.

"What is important is seldom urgent...and what is urgent is seldom important." - *Former President, Dwight D Eisenhower*

We have a natural tendency to want to do those things that *appear* to be urgent first, but they can eat up time and may not always be the most important.

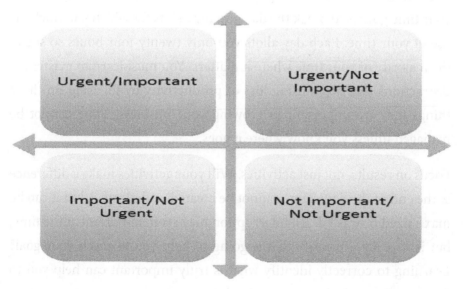

Urgent and Important. The first box is labeled "Urgent and Important." These are the activities that are considered a crisis or pressing problem. They can have a way of eating up the day if not managed carefully. Examples of "Urgent and Important" time thieves are deadline-driven items that could have been better planned, an urgent call from a major client about a problem project, or a printer breakdown when you are trying to get a proposal or report out the door. Spending too much time in this quadrant can cause stress and burnout. You feel that you are always in crisis management. Evaluate whether these items can be moved out of this quadrant with better planning or forecasting, or would be best delegated to someone else.

Urgent but Not Important. These tasks are the interruptions and distractions that are usually more important to someone else and can keep you from achieving your goals and completing your work. Examples include incoming phone calls, incoming texts, some committee meetings, and minor employee disputes. Spending too much time in this quadrant creates a short-term focus that causes you to feel out of control and at the mercy of other people's demands. Learn to say no. Try to reschedule or delegate these tasks.

Important but Not Urgent. Effective time managers spend the majority of their time focused on this quadrant in order to find the most value for time that is focused on growing their business. Here is where you should be spending 80 percent of your time. This is the quadrant of balance, and will include the daily tasks that put the groundwork in place for the future of your business. Address important matters in a measured way, before they become urgent. Examples include Business Development activities such as calling or visiting clients or prospects, working on proposals, or working on that strategic plan that is due in three months.

Not Important and Not Urgent. Tasks in this box are generally a waste of your time. They are trivial and will ultimately rob you of productive time that could be used to further the business. Examples include the majority of e-mails, busywork, web surfing, social media, chatting with office staff about non-business related topics. Get rid of those things that are not important and not urgent—or if they are essential to the business but you don't really have the interest, outsource the work. The money you pay to have someone else do the things you don't enjoy doing can be more than recouped if you will spend more time on Business Development activities—which fit into the "Important but Not Urgent" category.

Procrastination. Time management can be a challenge when we have too many things to do—a situation that can cause serious procrastination problems. The things you need to do may all be important, but each requires time and focus. The more important it is, the more likely procrastination will set in. The mind goes into overload and you end up doing nothing—which of course makes it worse. First, make sure you are clear on what needs to be done, and then try writing down the tasks required to complete the job. Prioritize the jobs according to their impact on the business. Label each job with the amount of time you expect it to take, and do as much as you can. Maybe you won't be able to complete a big task all at once, but when part of it is done it will be easier to pick it back up again.

Keep a Running To-Do List Based on Your Goals. Making a to-do list based on priorities can be a great time management tool. However, a problem can be created if the list is not kept current. It turns into a guilt list and becomes a list of things you think you *should* be doing, rather than a list of things that *will* get done. This then makes it difficult to identify the things that are most important to growing the business. The answer is to make intentional choices about what needs to be done and what can be ignored. If the item has been on the list for a while and is not getting done, discard it, delegate it—or if it's important for you to do it, then move it to a long-term focused list. Your daily to-do list should correspond to your overall business growth goals. When tasks are managed this way, the plan for growth is much more likely to become a reality. Your to-do list should always include the Business Development calls you want to make that day.

Value of Planning. Planning ahead is always smart time management and can become a habit with just a little practice. Manage the day, but keep your eye on long-term goals. Make a list of long-term things that need to be accomplished in order to meet your business plan—this becomes your road map. Your daily plan comes from this road map and will help you cut the clutter and allow you to focus on what really needs your attention. A road map is your frame of reference, and a daily plan can help with getting from point A to point B on that road map. It highlights key processes and checkpoints to ensure progress is being made, and will help to neutralize the "flavor of the week" stressful projects.

E-mail Overload. Don't be a slave to technology; it is intended to function as a support tool, not a master of your time. E-mail in particular can be a major time monster. It is a wonderful communication tool, but we must manage the overwhelming overload that this information exchange causes. One thing you can do to manage your inbox is to delete liberally. Of all the e-mail you receive in a day, 20 percent of them are probably worth 80 percent of the time you spend on e-mail. If it's not critical or the sender is not recognized, don't even open it. Trying to organize your inbox may be a waste of time because most e-mail programs now have search capabilities that allow you to find whatever you need. Delete freely—most likely, you can always get it again from somebody if you really need it.

Separate personal e-mail from business e-mail. Set up a different account to receive all of your personal correspondence. In addition, set up separate accounts to receive subscriptions such as newsletters and publications. That way you can view them when you have the time, and not allow them to interfere with your business focus.

Be careful about replying to all the e-mail you receive. You can keep conversation strings going without producing any constructive results. It may be best to politely close the string or just ignore it. Each e-mail response eats up about twenty minutes. By the time you open it and read it, consider the information, and then craft a response, you may well have used up twenty minutes of your valuable time. You have to decide if it's worth it to you. Consider delegating it to someone else to provide a response to the sender.

Another time-saving strategy for e-mail communication is to have a set time each day for checking your inbox. Continuously checking e-mail throughout the day is a serious distraction to what you are currently focused on doing. Block out times in your schedule to focus on e-mail, such as in the morning and before leaving the office, and go through them all at once. It will be easier to complete the task quickly, and will increase your ability to make better decisions about what's important.

Multi-tasking. Some people pride themselves on their ability to multi-task. In truth, it really does not work very well, and causes you to lose focus. You tend to create your own distractions when you multi-task. If a task is important enough to be on your to-do list, it must be important enough to focus on and complete before starting something else. Decide how much time you will allocate to focusing on the task at hand, and don't change that focus—no matter what—until it is complete. This takes discipline, but pays off by allowing you to work through your to-do list more quickly.

Do everything you can to avoid interruptions. Studies prove that when people are interrupted, they seldom go back to the task with the same level of interest and focus as before. The more challenging the task, the more likely they will not return to it at all, so it's best to control the interruptions. Some people like to give themselves a reward incentive to complete a task. It can be as simple as a snack or a walk around the office, but the purpose is to have something to look forward to when the job is complete.

Know the time of day when you can be most productive. Some people work best in the morning, and so that's when to plan those things that require the most focus and concentration. Understanding your biorhythms and planning your day around them can greatly enhance your productivity.

Stay Focused on What Matters. The ultimate goal is to stay keenly focused on those things that will make a difference to the business. When new ideas or business-increasing thoughts come along, you want to have the time available to focus on them immediately.

While it may not be necessary to react hastily when you have a new idea, don't lose valuable time, either. Act on it while the idea is hot and the emotion is strong—take action as soon as possible before the idea dims or the feeling passes.

Let's say that the intent is to organize a new marketing campaign. Begin the process immediately, while the intent is strong, by taking the first step. Call a meeting to discuss with staff and to make assignments. We intend to take action when the idea strikes us. We intend to do something when the emotion is strong, but if we don't translate that intention into *action* fairly soon, the urgency starts to diminish. Time is well spent when we begin the process immediately before the wisdom and intent is gone or diminished.

Time-stressors are the most pervasive source of pressure in the workplace, and will happen as a result of having too much to do and too little time to get it all done. When running a business, there never seems to be enough time to do all the things that need to be done. Realize that the workload is not going to change, but if goals and priorities are clearly defined and are allotted a specific amount of time in each work day, you will feel less overwhelmed and more in control of the success of the business.

Make sure you are focused on the right things and stop doing the things that do not affect results. Many time wasters can be delegated or ignored. Have you ever noticed how some things seem to work themselves out whenever we step away and allow it to happen? Stay focused on the end results and manage your time—don't allow it to manage you.

Key Concepts in this Chapter

1. Time is the most valuable resource in your business so it must be managed wisely.
2. Stay focused on what matters. Business Development efforts are important and should focus on results, not just activities.
3. Use a matrix to organize and rank activities according to how important or urgent they are and address them accordingly.
4. Multi-tasking is seldom effective.
5. Manage e-mail overload and do not allow it to manage you.
6. Rid yourself of time wasters as you go through the day.

17

WORKING FOR THE GOVERNMENT

As a small business, consider marketing your services to the government. The federal government, the state, counties, cities, and municipalities receive federal funding for projects that are specifically set aside for disadvantaged small businesses. This can be lucrative if your firm fits one of the many set-aside categories such as minority-owned, woman-owned, service-disabled veteran-owned, veteran-owned, or under a certain size. Your business may be located in a HubZone (Historically Under Utilized Business Zones). These categories receive preferential consideration by the selection committees when making project award decisions. The government has issued minimum percentage goals for disadvantaged firms when federal funds are involved. Some government entities find it difficult to meet these requirements because not enough disadvantaged businesses submit proposals.

Many small businesses feel that the process is difficult and time-consuming and so will choose to avoid the exercise entirely. This need not be the case. There is a paperwork process required in order for the government to show it is being a good steward of the taxpayers' dollars. While the paperwork can be intimidating, it is becoming more streamlined, and most agencies have professionals that are dedicated to helping you through the process. Just know that it will take some time to get set up, but in the end it may very well be worth it to your firm. Check the website of the agency you are interested in for posted opportunities and the names of the small business liaison staff that can help you.

Look at their list of contract holders and contact those firms where you have a relationship. If you want to test the waters first it might be worthwhile to team with a larger firm to help you learn the process for working with the government.

Visit the Small Business Administration (SBA) www.sba.gov and the General Services Administration (GSA) www.gsa.gov websites for pointers. These government agencies were set up to help small businesses succeed in procuring federal projects and will assist you with the process.

The SBA can help you determine if your business fits within a special category. They will help you to register on a central website set up so that the various agencies can search for the small companies that meet the particular requirements of their projects. To complete this process, you will need to know what North American Industry Classification System (NAICS) code your type of service fits into, because this is how you will be classified and how they will find you. It is also how you will search for opportunities that fit your firm's skill set. You may fit within more than one classification.

Check the various federal agencies' websites for their procurement forecast of upcoming projects. Set an appointment to talk with the managing departments to introduce yourself and your firm's capabilities. People still do business with people even in the government.

Local governments such as state, county and city governments will generally post their opportunities on their websites. Some states have a central location for business opportunities and require all entities to post in one location which makes the opportunities easier to find. It is easy to determine which have funding by the number of projects projected in their budget—this is all public information. Get to know the decision-makers before the RFP is released to the public. Once it is released as an RFP, they are not allowed to talk about it with you.

Federal opportunities are posted on a free website, Federal Business Opportunities, at www.FedBizOps.gov. You can register using your NAICS code to receive notifications when opportunities are posted that are a good fit for your business.

How Is the Federal Government Procurement Process Organized? It is not really as daunting as it may seem—it's just different from business in general. The federal government purchases supplies and services in accordance with the Federal Acquisition Regulation (FAR). The FAR contains the procurement rules and processes that all federal agencies must follow for acquisitions from one to hundreds of millions of dollars.

The procurement organizations are aligned along the major agencies: Departments of Defense, Homeland Security, Agriculture, Transportation, and so forth.

Federal agencies can also purchase supplies and services through schedules managed by the General Services Administration (GSA). A GSA schedule is a good beginning for a small business. GSA operates and maintains most of the federal buildings and so it will have thousands of projects each year. They are required to consider small business capabilities first. Just be aware that it takes time to negotiate rates and schedules (contracted rates) but once these are set up, the hard part is done. The GSA hosts a dedicated website listing opportunities under a set amount (currently $25,000) which can only be accessed by their existing schedule holders. The GSA does not automatically award work to their contract holders—you still have to submit proposals.

The federal government may seem big and impersonal, but each individual procurement action must be accomplished by a contracting officer who is responsible for the legal aspects of the purchase. This person is authorized by the federal government to commit tax dollars for the procurement. Each agency or department will have multiple contracting officers responsible for these actions. It is important to know the contracting officer and agency responsible for the procurements that are of interest to your firm. Go see them. Even though it is the federal government, people still buy from people. If they need your service, they will help guide you through the process.

Government and commercial buyers behave the same—most will choose the path of least resistance, so make it easy for them to see the value you provide. Price isn't everything; federal buyers view obtaining the best value for the taxpayer as a noble objective, but in the end their own promotions or raises for well-managed projects will come first. Most people are motivated by self-interest. That's not necessarily a bad thing; it's just the way it is. Having a clear picture of the various roles of the people in the federal market will help you to better target your Business Development efforts.

The largest buyer of goods and services in the world is the Department of Defense (DoD). DoD procurements are performed by the individual services (such as the Army, Navy, Air Force, and Marine Corps) and by the Defense Logistics Agency (DLA). The DLA procures goods and services that are common to all the services, such as fuel, construction materials, common supplies, and some vehicles. The individual services also procure their common supplies and services as necessary. Major Military Construction (MILCON) procurements are performed predominantly by the Army and the Navy. Army construction acquisitions are managed by the US Army Corps of Engineers (USACE). The Navy acquisitions are managed by the Naval Facilities Engineering Command (NAVFAC). USACE and NAVFAC serve the major construction requirements of the

Air Force and Marine Corps, depending on the installation's location in the continental United States and overseas.

The **US Army Corps of Engineers (USACE)** is responsible for contracting and managing major construction requirements for the Army, Air Force, Coast Guard, and several other agencies. If you want to go after large projects, get to know people in divisions in your area.

(1) The North Atlantic Division (NAD) is located in New York. The Baltimore and Norfolk Districts are assigned to NAD. Know the commanders for each district that you want to market.

(2) The South Atlantic Division (SAD) is located in Atlanta. The Savannah, Jacksonville, and Mobile Districts are assigned to SAD.

Director of Public Works (DPW). Each Army installation has a DPW, who is in charge of the facilities and infrastructure. This would include all master planning, repair, and new work under the MILCON.

New work over a certain amount (currently $750,000) is handled by the geographical Army Corps of Engineers district headquarters nearest to the military installation. The DPW master planner works as a team with the district program manager's team to develop the project(s).

The Naval Facilities Engineering Command (NAVFAC) is responsible for major construction requirements for the Navy and Marine corps installations in the continental United States and at select locations overseas. NAVFAC also oversees major construction and facilities-related procurements for the Air Force, Coast Guard, and other agencies depending on location and mission.

Public Works Departments (PWD). Most Navy and Marine Corps installations have a Public Works Department (PWD) that performs the day-to-day facilities operations including planning, maintenance, repair, and minor construction services. Nearly all the Navy PWDs have been incorporated into the Regional NAVFAC operation.

New work for large projects is handled by the Regional NAVFAC HQ responsible for that military installation. The PWD master planner works as a team with the Regional NAVFAC program manager's team to develop the project(s).

The best way to make a federal or state government sale is to talk with them directly. Talk to the end users, the contracting departments, the regional heads, and anyone necessary in order to become known. While their hands are tied when it comes to certain regulations and requirements, they still want to buy from people and firms they know and trust. Their success and future promotions depend on getting the best people to do the work. The decision-makers want to get the best deals that work for them and their superiors. Always keep in mind that risk mitigation is a major factor when it comes to government work. Help them to make informed decisions by showing them that your firm is strong, capable, and financially stable.

Develop Relationships with these Typical Management Positions:

- small business liaison
- technical division directors
- director of contracting or procurement
- director of operations/construction/engineering or your firm's area of expertise

Special Rules in Dealing with Government Employees and Directors

- Be very careful about offering freebies, trips, or events of any value to government employees. They are not allowed to accept gifts of any kind, nor can they have their meals paid for by private firms.

To do so could cause them to lose their jobs or face charges of bribery. Just avoid it and save yourself embarrassment.

- There is a distinct relationship between civilian directors and military commanders when it comes to the procurement and contracting process. It's OK to ask for clarification.
- Military commanders are in charge of USACE organizations overall, but civilian directors run selection panels and write specs for RFPs.

There are a number of professional associations that are attended by federal government employees—it's a good idea to attend as a way of meeting them. Check with other professional services firms in your type of business to see what organizations they are attending that provides opportunities to meet government employees. Listed are a few suggestions for the Architect/Engineering/Construction (A/E/C) industry:

- The **American Council of Engineering Companies (ACEC)** provides opportunities at the state and national level to engage federal officials on issues related to engineering companies.
- The **Association of Defense Communities (ADC)** is the leading membership organization supporting communities with active, closed, and closing defense installations. Consider joining and use the newsletters to learn about opportunities in these communities.
- The **Army Engineer Association (AEA)** provides opportunities to communicate with the leaders of the Army Corps of Engineers at the local installations.
- **Construction Management Association of America (CMAA).** As a result of CMAA's efforts, several federal agencies have become very involved in organizations such as CMAA and support the Certified Construction Manager (CCM) Program. Many federal agencies,

particularly the US Postal Service and General Services Administration, promote the use of CCMs in their construction solicitations.

- The **Design-Build Institute of America (DBIA)** promotes the education and training of those involved in this process. A large number of Department of Defense construction-related contracts are awarded through the Design-Build method.

- The **Green Building Council (GBC)** manages the Leadership in Energy and Environmental Design (LEED) accreditation and certification process. Many federal agencies are requiring LEED certification for their new and existing facilities, and are looking for LEED-accredited professionals to be on their professional service contracts.

- The **Society of American Military Engineers (SAME)** is an important professional organization to participate in, both at the local posts and at the national level. The post locations are normally near large military installations and district locations.

- **The Infrastructure Security Partnership (TISP)** was formed immediately after 9/11 to provide information and feedback on the nation's most critical infrastructure. Many federal agencies and professional associations are represented within the partnership.

The federal government is a very large and complex owner. To effectively market a specific agency or department, you must know the agency requirements, the rules associated with the spending of their funds, and the contract methods they prefer to use to execute those funds.

Working for government does require going through a lengthy registration process but as a small business you owe it to yourself to explore this opportunity. It is not necessary to pay a consultant to do this for you—it is all public information and there are public agencies to help you. Yes, there is competition in the federal market but there is competition in all areas of business. A targeted approach that selectively identifies agencies and departments of interest is critical to maintaining a high degree of success when pursuing government—especially federal—opportunities. The federal and military market is not easy to break into, but once credibility is established, this market can sustain a firm for many years.

Key Concepts in this Chapter

1. Small professional services firms can benefit from working for the government.
2. Certain categories receive preferential treatment by decision makers for government projects.
3. While the qualification process may seem intimidating, and requires paper work, it is not difficult.
4. Most agencies have people whose job it is to help you through the process.
5. Even though it's the government, people still buy from people.
6. In order to meet the right people, it helps to network and become involved with the various organizations that focus on government.

18

INTERNAL BUSINESS DEVELOPMENT MEETINGS

Part of effectively managing the Business Development effort is conducting regular meetings to discuss progress and planning. Don't tack these discussions onto the end of an operations meeting. Give them a stand-alone time slot because it is a separate focus. Whether you have one employee or three hundred, Business Development–focused meetings can be very effective in creating a *team* mindset within the group. Although many tasks related to selling the firm's services will be done individually, a regular meeting provides the opportunity for people to come together to support each other and to discuss goals and achievements.

People tend to resist meetings because they fail to see the value of taking the time out of their busy schedules—and everyone is busy. As the leader of the group, your job is to make sure the information exchange is useful and relevant and that everyone feels they are receiving a return on the time invested. The key is to meet regularly and make it a priority. *Expect* people to participate, and let them know that you expect them to attend and participate.

Good Reasons for a Meeting. A good reason for holding a meeting is when you need to track progress, set goals, or to make a critical decision.

Make sure those people attending are critical to the discussion. Another reason to hold a meeting would be that you want to gather input and have a discussion where ideas bounce off each other, as in a brainstorming fashion.

The Wrong Reasons for a Meeting. Sometimes organizations have so many meetings that it makes it difficult to get any work done. Is the meeting really necessary or is it a waste of time? How do you know if the meeting is a bad idea? The following may be some of those situations.

- To give a report. If you are meeting to give a report that can be made in the form of an electronic communication, then there is no need to get everyone together. Almost any type of report can be sent to a number of people at once to share information.
- To enforce a deadline. Some people set up meetings to assure a deadline or timeline is met. This may be a cultural problem. Deadlines can be kept without getting everyone in a room at the same time.

When making a decision about the need to have a meeting, consider whether the benefit is worth the cost of the time for the people attending. If you can't say that it is, then it may not be necessary to have the meeting in the first place.

Business Development Discussions should be considered a good reason to hold a meeting. It is imperative to Business Development efforts and for the company that your group comes together periodically. It lends a structure to the Business Development effort, and is how the group becomes a team. Staff will enjoy several benefits when the Business Development meeting is well run. The meeting can be a mechanism for the group to:

- communicate and share information
- mutually support each other

- track progress and hold each other accountable
- showcase successes
- bolster morale when losses occur
- motivate and empower each other

If managed well, a meeting need not be long and drawn out. The best way to control the meeting is to have someone in charge that directs the effort and keeps track of the time. This person needs to be able to maintain the focus by saying to a person who is trying to derail progress, "Thank you for your contribution," and then move on to the next item.

A good meeting will have the following components:

1. **An agenda** that outlines objectives and is circulated *before* the meeting. This allows participants to prepare for the meeting. It also gives them the opportunity to contribute what they would like to have discussed at the meeting.
2. **A set date.** Whether you decide to hold your Business Development meetings weekly or monthly, a preset meeting schedule allows everyone to plan ahead. The meeting is placed on the calendar, and nothing short of an emergency changes the time.
3. **A set start and end time.** Nothing is worse than to have a meeting that runs on and on because the leader cannot control those who like to hear themselves talk.
4. **A recorder who keeps notes.** Have someone take notes and capture what everyone says they plan to do. It is a good idea to circulate these notes so that everyone is reminded of their assigned tasks for the time period.
5. **End with a clear set of action items**. At the end of the meeting, the leader should review the action items and new assignments. The leader must confirm that attendees understand what they are to accomplish before the next meeting. The last item is to motivate and give the group their charge for the time period. Create some excitement!

What to Discuss. Talk about projects that have been won. This sets the stage to motivate everyone and to give the person that brought in the opportunity some limelight. Be sure to give credit to everybody who had anything to do with it at all. Encourage the team to give credit to others and to share success. Ask each participant to talk about the progress they have made on their assigned targets using the Client Capture Plan form (chapter 8).

The manager of the account should talk about the steps that have been accomplished and the plans to approach the next step in the process. Others can offer insights or information that might be helpful. If you choose to have marketing participate in this meeting, you might have a segment on the progress of proposals and the marketing effort. Make every effort to not allow the meeting to become sidetracked with operational issues—stay focused on Business Development.

Make It Fun! To keep the meetings interesting, you may want to have a contest or include a short educational element to the meetings. You can ask a project manager to highlight a new project or a technical subject. This educates those responsible for Business Development, helping them to understand the range of capabilities the company has to offer.

Remember to celebrate successes and to thank members of the team for their efforts. You might consider a contest or group outing as a reward when goals are reached. You could have both short-term and long-term reward plans. A commission-structured compensation plan may not work in some companies is because Business Development should be approached as a team effort. Technical professionals should be brought in at the appropriate time, and everyone in the company should work toward winning the project.

Different Personality Types. Be aware that when you are running the meeting, there will be many personality types involved and some of them can be negative. Human nature becomes interesting during these meetings; the trick is to turn them around so there is less negative impact to the entire group. Sometimes you can find a positive way to spin the behavior to benefit from the traits of such personalities. As leader of the meeting you must be aware and control such behaviors. Here are a few negative personality types that the leader of the group may be required to deal with:

- **The Self-Important Person**. This is the person who says he or she does not have time to attend—he or she is just too busy. It could be that people like this really are busy, but it probably means they are not prepared or have not done what they should have been doing. Those who are doing what they should are always anxious to share what they have accomplished.

- **The Pusher.** Another variation of this is the person who tells you— before the meeting—that it must be over by a certain time because he or she has important things to do. During the meeting pushers will make remarks like, "Let's move on," or "Do we really need to discuss that now?" Interestingly, what you will find is that when it is their turn to speak, they have all the time in the world!

- **The Bully—the Know-It-All**. This person tries to speak louder than anyone else and tends to run over those that are less boisterous. This personality type disagrees with ideas presented by others just for the sake of being adversarial. Bullies make others feel their ideas are stupid, and may actually say as much. The problem with this type is that others in the group stop talking or contributing, for fear of being made to feel inferior or less knowledgeable. As the leader of the meeting, you must be strong enough to confront this behavior and show how it impacts the group. If you let them get away with it, it will just get worse. Lay some ground rules such as not allowing interruptions or put-downs. Never allow comments to be personalized. Insist that everyone be treated with respect and consideration at your meetings. If the person is a superior and you find that he or she cannot be controlled, make an effort to return to the person that was put down and ask for his or her input at another time during the meeting. Hopefully, your point will be taken that everyone's input is of value.

- **The Sidetracker.** This is the person who thinks that what he or she has to say is more important than the agenda. These people want to be heard immediately and have no regard for the plan or organization for the discussion. You may need to interrupt by saying, "Joe, that's an interesting point. Let's table that for future discussion and get back to our agenda so that we can stick to our schedule." This is why it is important to have a set time frame for meetings. You can always control the sidetracked discussion by calling people back to the agenda in order to stick to your time frame.

- **The Philosopher.** This person wants to gain attention or control by throwing out philosophical questions like, "What if we could double our revenue?" Of course, everyone stops to hear what philosophers have to say. The problem is that by the time they get their point across, and you realize it is of no value, you've wasted a lot of time. They just want to pontificate! If there is not value to the attempt to sidetrack the discussion, it is your responsibility to bring the meeting back to the immediate focus. You must be able to do that out of respect for everybody's time.

- **The Rambler** is the person that makes some good points but it takes forever to articulate what he or she has to say. Each bit of good information ramblers contribute is surrounded with so much fluff that what should be a single sentence can take twenty minutes to come across. Control this by politely asking a question that cuts to the chase.

- **The Questioner** is the person who asks questions while someone is talking in order to appear intelligent or very attentive. An occasional question may be OK, but too many can be distracting to the speaker and the direction of the conversation. You might offer time for questions at the end, or point out that the information will be covered later on the agenda. What you will generally find is that questioners will not have questions when you ask for them—only when they want to direct the attention to themselves and away from the speaker.

When it becomes obvious that certain people are bound to be a disruption and will not discuss change, you may want to consider not including them in your meetings. Keep in mind that most people don't even realize they are an annoyance, and so it may be worthwhile to respectfully point out the issue to them in a private setting. As the leader, it is your job to control the meeting and the personalities. However, you must remain flexible. Sometimes in an attempt to stick to the agenda and the timing, you may miss items that could be beneficial to the group.

Continuously remind the group that the Business Development meeting is focused on tracking progress and on setting goals and targets. It is intended to track and discuss opportunities that can increase revenue. While activities are good to discuss, the real purpose of the meeting is to stay focused on results and the true opportunities.

Key Concepts in this Chapter

1. Conducting effective Business Development meetings are important because it provides an opportunity to determine priorities, track progress, and discuss various options for gaining new business opportunities.
2. The Business Development meeting has a different focus and should not be made part of an operations meeting.

3. Have a clear agenda, a set timeframe, and a recurring date so that people can plan their schedules around the meeting.

4. Keep the meeting topics relevant, interesting and fun. Do not allow personality types to derail the discussion.

19

FINAL WORDS

As the owner of a small business, your goal should be to work *on* your business, not *in* it. You owe it to your employees to grow the business into a strong and viable operation that provides a stable work environment for many years. When you are busy working in the business on a day-to-day basis, you will end up doing activities that lead you astray from your real business goals. Engaging in the genuine discipline of growing the business requires that you develop the ability to set goals and take action.

Spend time on planning. The world is too competitive to leave the growth of your company to chance. Think about where you need to be in six months, and make sure you are aligning your focus and activities with that goal.

Understand what truly differentiates your business from those of your competitors, and invest more resources into highlighting that part of the business. Know the best clients for your skill set and go where they are so that you can meet and interact with them. Form relationships with the intent that you will be working with these people for many years to come.

Allow people to help you. We are all born with the natural urge to help one another. If clients are happy with the work your firm provides, they will be glad to refer others to you. They may not think of it unless you ask, so let people know how they can help you in your business.

You may want to hire a business or sales coach to guide you and hold you accountable for accomplishing what you want to do. Train and mentor your professional staff on how to help grow the business. The payoff is exponential as they gather experience and teach others.

Pay it forward. I hope you've gleaned some useful information from this book that will make a difference in growing your business. I want to encourage you to help others by sharing what you've learned. You will benefit from the teaching experience as it reinforces what you've learned, but it will also help someone else. And that's how the world becomes a better place—one person at a time helping another.

As much as I've enjoyed sharing this information with you, I want you to know that you will only learn by *doing* and not just by reading. You may feel that all this information makes sense and you understand Business Development after reading about it, but you will only understand at a superficial level. When you apply what you've learned, and actually experience it for yourself, is when you will gain a deeper level of understanding.

Law of Diminishing Intent. To avoid falling victim to the law of diminishing intent, take action now while the desire is strong. If after reading this book, you want to improve upon your current Business Development program or initiate a new program—translate that intention into action right away. Take the first step and call a meeting of key people in the firm to discuss and then plan the next step. When that's underway, plan the next step, and so on. If you fail to translate the intention into action soon, the urgency is lost. When that happens, you've just read another book containing interesting information—that failed to make a change in your life.

Knowledge must be coupled with action in order to make a difference. By forming the discipline to take action, you set off a chain reaction that can cause a significant and positive impact on your business.

Having the discipline to take action creates a wonderful feeling of control, and the sense of self-worth and self-esteem that you allow yourself and your staff is priceless. Start with the smallest discipline that corresponds to your goals and take action. Make the commitment: "I will discipline myself to achieve my goals so that in the years ahead I can celebrate my success!"

You have all the knowledge you need to build a successful business, but the only way to grow and to really be successful is to work at it continually. A small amount of time each day dedicated to Business Development creates the "magic."

Aristotle said, "It's not the knowledge…but the *action* that creates the power"!

Key Concepts in this Chapter

1. Work on growing your business and do not allow it to control you.
2. Commit to dedicate time each day toward Business Development.
3. You now have the knowledge but it is only effective when put into *action*.
4. Help others and allow them to help you.
5. Start immediately to apply what you've learned while the intent is high.

You are invited to visit my website for additional information at www. SpurlockConsulting.com.